G O I N G
SOLO

LEVELING THE PLAYING FIELD IN PROFESSIONAL SERVICES

James Voigt

ISBN 978-1-63630-772-5 (Paperback)
ISBN 978-1-63630-773-2 (Hardcover)
ISBN 978-1-63630-774-9 (Digital)

Covenant Books, Inc.
11661 Hwy 707
Murrells Inlet, SC 29576
www.covenantbooks.com

To my wife, and to every other spouse who had the guts to just say okay when the thought of a regular paycheck is about to go out the window.

ACKNOWLEDGMENTS

It's an amazing thing when you tell your wife that you're going to quit your swanky downtown law firm job and open your own shop, and she doesn't miss a beat and says okay. Then you tell her you're going to write a book about it and take a shot at being a writer, and once again, she says okay. Of course, this all comes almost twenty years after saying you'd like to finish undergrad and go to law school with a brand-new baby to care for, and she says—you guessed it—okay.

My wife is a woman of few words, but she means what she says, and she has always supported every move I've made (even the crazy ones).

I also need to thank Don Kiolbassa, who had been begging me to go solo for years before I finally had the guts to do it, and he definitely showed me that you can thrive on your own, both personally and professionally. Don has also been an incredibly valuable support system, cheerleader, mentor, and all-around amazingly good guy. Don's faith in my abilities as an attorney has been a cornerstone of my success ever since going solo.

Thank you to Carolyn Selke, who means what she says when she tells you she believes in you. She's an incredibly strong survivor and one of the most giving people you'll ever meet.

Thank you to Keven and Kim Bennema. Your confidence in me made this leap possible.

Thank you to Ami Castaneda, who had this insane thought that if I was going to tell people I was writing a book, I should actually write it. Thank you to her husband, Jim Ellis, for always reminding me that I have something important to say.

Thank you to my writing coach, Chuck Scharenberg, for unscrambling my brain to the point that I could actually get this book done on time. Well, almost on time. Chuck accomplished the nearly impossible task of convincing me that I'm not a giant disaster of a human being; I just needed a few tweaks to work in a way that works for me.

No acknowledgement would be complete without thanking my parents. You'll never meet three people (it's complicated) more genuinely interested in what their kiddo has to say. And for making the very Mom-like suggestion to clean up the language of this book. That's the most Mom-like suggestion anyone could make. And shoot, Mom was right again.

And in a very weird way (again it's complicated), I need to thank my stepfather, who went solo when I was still in high school and showed me that it's possible even if you've got some...flaws. I'll leave it at that.

THAT NAGGING VOICE IN YOUR HEAD IS PROBABLY RIGHT

Going solo is not for everyone. I don't mean that in a bravado "you can't handle the hustle" kind of way. I simply mean that there are three paths to follow in service-based industries like the law. You can simply be an employee, earn a good salary, and make a nice profit for your boss. You can pursue the partnership route where the employee path eventually leads to you being the boss (or at least one of the bosses), or you can do what I did: look it all in the face and chuck it; open your own tiny little corner of the world and go solo.

It's not really that some people can't handle going solo; it's just that some people may not like it. However, the fact that you picked up this book at all makes me suspect you're one of us.

There are some people whose thoughts continually return to the question of what it would be like to be on their own. To make their own rules. To set their own dress code and schedule. To treat clients the way they think clients should be treated, and to be perfectly blunt, there are some of us who are simply not willing to bow at the throne of partnership and humbly request the right to kiss the ring and spend hundreds of thousands of dollars for the opportunity to be a minority owner of a business you might be able to replicate entirely on your own. No, thanks.

If you're picking up a not-so-slight hint of attitude in that last run-on sentence, and you're liking it a little bit, then this book is probably for you. And that chip on your shoulder, that slight (or severe) disdain for being told what to do makes you exceptionally well-suited to going solo.

However, the question that really matters is this: Can you pull it off? Can you actually walk away from a consistent bi-weekly salary, probably a decent bonus, health insurance, open-bar firm outings, secretary, a nice office with a view, and toss it all to literally start from nothing and do it all on your own? If all of that sounds fairly overwhelming but curiously and inexplicably attractive to you, then keep reading. If not, and you're knocking down good pay and like the people you work with, then by all means, keep your well-paying gig.

There's nothing wrong with having a regular job. It's just that it drives some of us nuts for no apparent reason, and we need out. The chapters of this book were my way out.

I'm here to talk to the ones who can't stop looking out the window. The ones who can't stand staring out the window on the train into the city. The ones who have about had it with telling their kids they can't get home in time to see their dance class. The ones who are done missing the Christmas pageant at school or simply sick of not having time to have a real conversation with their little ones before it's time to rush off to bed and do it all again the next day. I'm writing to the ones whose book of business is barely enough to keep the boss off your back but would actually be a pretty decent income if it was just your revenue. This book is for the ones who find themselves wondering time and time again, "Could I really resign? Would I survive? Could I handle it?" Yes. Yes. And yes. You can do this.

If any of the opening lines of this chapter hit home for you, then you are the reason I wrote this book. And the good news is that I've succeeded enough, screwed enough of it up, and interviewed enough other solos that I can steer you around the mistakes and save you the trouble of making them yourself. I've done some of it right and some of it wrong. And coming through it all, I look at my life, and I am incredibly blessed to be living a life I genuinely love living. I don't sit around drinking umbrella drinks all day in cargo shorts; this is hard work, but it's hard work that I'm doing only thirty-nine feet away from my bedroom door. I'm doing it while never missing dinner with my wife and kids. I'm doing it a way that is making my clients happier than they've ever been. And I'm doing it at a lower cost to them while putting more into my own pocket than I ever have before. This is a good life. And the entire purpose of this book is to tell you that you can have whatever you call a good life too.

I love that I was able to design my own solo life. Going solo can be like Instagram start-up entrepreneurial star Gary Vaynerchuck with a nonstop hustle at 4:30 a.m. for eighteen hours every day, seven days a week grind that makes you shockingly wealthy. Or maybe that doesn't suit you. So instead, it can be a good solid income that gives you the freedom to spend all the time you want with your family. Or somewhere in the middle. You pick. You decide which path you want. And here's the best part: if you decide you don't like the path you picked, there is no partnership committee that you need to convince to change course. You just change course because you want to, simply because you want to. The only requirement is that you absolutely must deliver value to your clients and your family. But how you do that is 100 percent up to you. This is the freedom I have today.

We're going to talk numbers in this book, so let's get it out in the open. I have designed my business to generate around $300,000 to $400,000 in annual income for me and my family to enjoy. That's my mark, the center of the goalposts for the lifestyle I've chosen. Sometimes I kick it right down the middle. Other times, I hit the upright. And other times, well, let's just say I have definitely given up the lifestyle of someone whose paycheck is exactly the same every other Friday. This is a roller coaster. But when you're the one driving it, it doesn't feel nearly as chaotic as being an employee/passenger and hanging on for dear life, hoping to God that management doesn't shift in the wind and start firing people.

I've made the conscious decision to work less and be around for my family more. A lot more. Not because it's *right*—I'm not here to judge your decisions on what your income should be—but because I chose to focus more on family than income because it's what I want to do. When I started, I walked my eleven-year-old daughter to the bus every morning (she's too old for that now). Every single morning, before she walks out that door, she says I love you, and I'm there to say it right back. And that, to me, is worth more than any amount of income.

That is solid gold for me at this point in my life. That's not going to last forever, but while it's there, I'm soaking up every ounce of it. And tomorrow night, I'm closing the office early so I can see my older daughter's cheer showcase, a minor event at their practice facility, not even a competition, but it's important to her, so I'm going. I didn't even have to submit any forms to HR, and I didn't have to e-mail my managing partner; I just decided to close the office to be with my family because I wanted to.

I've cooked dinner for my family almost every night for the last two weeks (although they may dispute this being a "benefit" of going solo), and we've started going to church again every week.

This is my utopia. I chose the family-first plan. I could make more money. However, where I come from, $300,000 a year is a solid income. I have no complaints, but having been solo for a while now, I know for a fact that I could explode that income if I made different choices, put in longer hours, stepped away from the family more, and jumped into the hustle and grind culture you see so many posts about on Instagram. I could punch it up to $500,000 or even $1,000,000 if I made the right moves. And for some people, that's the right path. But the point is that by going solo, you instantly gain the flexibility to pursue whatever goal you want for yourself, to decide first what lifestyle you want, and then design a work plan that gets you there. You will never again define your life by what you can fit around the edges of what your employer expects of you and is willing to pay you.

So let me ask you, has this idea of going solo been nagging at you? Every few months, do you at least take a second to wonder what it would be like? Have you mentioned to your spouse once or twice that it would be interesting to think about going solo but then you cast it aside because it's too pie in the sky? Then read this book.

I'm no superstar. I have plenty of flaws, and I have made a lot of mistakes, but I'm here and I'm providing for my family, and it's working. That's enough for me. It should also be enough to encourage you to take a few serious steps in the direction you've probably been called to for a long, long time.

In this book, you're going to learn about the steps you can take over the next twelve months or more to get ready to go solo. You're going to learn how to quit the right way and how I quit the wrong way, and still regret it. You're going to learn how to ethically secure your clients when you quit your job and generate ridiculous client loyalty to ensure they follow you. You're going to learn about generating a book of business that helps you hit your financial goal without breaking your back. You're going to learn the value of getting help, when to do it and how. And you're going to learn the right way to measure your success (hint: it's not money).

Enough of the small talk; it's time to get to work.

THE ISLAND OF MISFIT TOYS

I've always struggled in a traditional job, but I've been able to absolutely thrive since going out on my own. I think there are a lot of people out there like me. Either we don't fit in at work or we're just not thriving under the goals that our jobs have for us. But we know we're good at the craft. We know we can do the work, and do it well, but something just isn't clicking. That was me for more than twenty years, and in the end, by going solo, I found freedom. And I want to tell you how I did it so you can find freedom too.

I am not on a crusade to convince everyone to go solo. My crusade is to reach those who want to go solo but are afraid to try to pull it off or those who simply don't know how to make the transition. This book is not a practical guide to running a solo practice. There are dozens of books on the market to tell you the basics of running a law firm. I know that because I read them all. They were dry and did little else than state the patently obvious. "You need a billing system." "You should keep your personal and business finances separate." "Don't forget to get good insurance." Thanks, Captain Obvious. I'll take it from here. Oh, by the way, how do I ensure my personal finances don't implode?

What I didn't read and couldn't find and didn't even know that I needed was a book on how to go about walking out on a good job and starting from scratch or, more accurately, how to do all of that *without* starting from scratch. How do you go solo without running a Samurai sword through your personal finances until you finally figure out how to bring in business, bill, and collect? Is it possible to avoid that massive dip where you're living off savings for eighteen months (or more!) and hoping to God that you can at least match what your comfy salary used to be? There was no book for that, and if there was, I wouldn't be surprised if it caused a bit of controversy. You're teaching people how to walk out on their job after all. However, I see it differently. I wrote this book specifically to teach the average, beaten-down associate or partner how to build themselves up to the point that they can walk out on their well-paying job if that's what they want to do. That's likely to make some employers a bit more than irritated. It's likely that this book will be criticized for interfering with the employee-employer relationship, stirring the pot. I may be accused of being a troublemaker, but I'm okay with all of that because my mission is not to avoid offending employers in the legal industry; my mission is to level the playing field between employer and employee.

If someone does everything I recommend in this book and their employer recognizes their achievements and treats them accordingly, they won't quit. The only difference after doing so is that the employee will forever have that option. And to be honest, employers don't necessarily like that.

If you build yourself up to the point that you have a solid book of business that will follow you wherever you go, the ability to bill at strong hourly rates and collect from clients who love working with you, then you have effectively levelled the playing field with your boss. Your boss, if you happen to have one right now, can fire you at any moment. I know this personally. I've been fired. It's not at all fun. They can pull the rug out from under your life without a moment's notice in most states. What leverage do you have that comes anywhere close to that atom bomb on your life? Likely, none.

Sure you could quit. Your boss will immediately get on the phone with all of your clients, assign all of your pending projects to other attorneys, and your departure will be little more than a bump in the road...for them. For you, you just lost your sole source of income and need to either get another job ASAP or start digging up clients fast (and hope they pay). So you just go into work every day, hoping to produce enough and say the right things at meetings so that you don't get fired. You hope to God that something insane, like a fight among the partners, doesn't eventually split up the firm or just shut it down entirely.

But what if the playing field was level? What if you had the ability to transition into solo practice at any moment, and doing so wouldn't be tantamount to dropping a grenade into your 401(k) portfolio? What if you were working at your job in exactly the way you could be working on your own, and it was working? Then something magical happens.

When the playing field is level between you and your employer, you only stay if you enjoy working at your job. You only stay if you don't mind the commute. You only stay if you receive the respect you deserve for the skills that you have. Your employer is expected to provide an environment that rewards you just like you are expected to provide work that rewards your employer.

Level playing field? Mission accomplished. If things go well, you'll stay at your job, and everyone is happy. If not, then you have the ability to take the momentum you've built up, the habits you've developed, the skills you've learned and simply keep doing those things as a solo. You won't be in the disadvantageous position of just starting to figure these things out after you've gone solo.

The focus of every other book out there on going solo in any field are the administrative details to running an office, but no one addresses the giant elephants in the room that are the sole focus on this book. My goal is that your practice will be so strong and so portable that the minor details addressed in most books on this topic will be little more than a passing thought because you've mastered the keys to thriving on your own. So if you're still making lists of the pros and cons of your top three alternatives for a billing system six months after going out on your own, you're failing. It's an indication that you haven't mastered the essentials, and that you're making yourself feel productive by focusing on more manageable details. That may sound harsh, but going solo is one of the most brutally honest mirrors you'll ever look into. In contrast, if you're bringing in $25,000 to $35,000 each month, you're really not going to care how much your credit card processing fees are costing you.

A good friend of mine went solo shortly after I did, and he struggled for a long time with whether to accept credit cards. He was concerned about the fees and hadn't gone through the very wide variety of different services available. In fairness, it's a lot to sort through. But as a solo, you have only one boss to make happy, and that's your clients. I told him that clients love paying by credit card, and that was the end of my analysis. Of course it cost money to accept credit cards. But every business has to spend at least something to make their customers or clients happy. And other than a few of these details, our overhead was ridiculously low, so we shouldn't complain about little things like credit card processing fees. We should be thankful that we're not spending tens or hundreds of thousands of dollars on maintaining equipment, etc. Which credit card system did I pick? *Not sure. Whatever one came with the billing system, I use.* How much am I paying in processing fees? *I have no idea. I've literally never seen a statement.* Why so cavalier about credit card fees? Because they represent less than one percent of my overall revenue. The solution to minor and annoying expenses is not to spend time trying to reduce them; the key is to boost your revenue to the point that they don't matter.

Most people, and most books on this topic, focus on the most inconsequential details when going solo, like which billing system to use, which e-mail provider, which malpractice insurance carrier, what kind of paper to use for their letterhead. The fact of the matter is that you should be thriving regardless of which billing system you chose and which credit card processor you selected because those are not the key factors to succeeding on your own. Focusing on these issues feels important because you're at least making decisions about *something*. However, these don't even rise to the level of details when it comes to going solo. They are the sub-details of issues that really don't matter. If your practice wins or loses because of a difference on the percentage your credit card processor charges you, then you're in a lot of trouble. I've spent more time writing about these topics in this book than I did making the various selections when I started on my own.

Focus on the issues that move the needle in radical ways. Focus on what matters when it comes to transforming yourself and your family into what you dream your life could be. What matters is generating ridiculous client loyalty and producing an income that is probably triple what you think you need to survive. What matters is mastering the ability to connect with people and knock down business reliably and consistently over and over again. What matters is mastering a specific and focused craft to the point that you can bill rates that reflect your genuine value to your clients.

These are the topics covered in this book. If you want a treatise on which brand of dry erase markers to use, there are plenty of those books out there on those topics. However, none of them are going to help you find freedom; they'll just help you feel like you're managing your office duties almost as well as your office manager did when you had a regular job. In the back of your mind, you know that there is a gaping hole in your plans to go solo, and it has nothing to do with which brand of paper clips you buy. The thing that keeps you from making the leap is the dread of falling flat on your face.

In the process of writing this book, I identified that the number one reason people don't leave a job they hate is because they cannot fathom making the leap to solo life. "Sure, if I had $300,000 of revenue from clients, of course I could leave!" "Sure, if I had three or four new clients coming in every month, of course I could leave." "Sure, if I knew my clients were going to come with me, I would leave."

What is your list of "Sure, if this was true" items? That list is different for everyone. But the bottom line is that most people probably feel like they could make it on their own if they could just survive the jump from employment into the great abyss of the entrepreneurial lifestyle. It scares the living hell out of them, so they just keep getting on that 5:52 train to the city every morning and getting back on the 6:07 train home every night (if they're lucky). And maybe they totally don't hate it, but they certainly don't love it.

I'm here to tell you that loving the practice of law is well within your reach, and this book is going to teach you how to make that leap and land squarely on your feet. You're going to look over your list of "Sure, if" items and put them into place now *while you're still at a job*. That's what I did well, and it's the main reason I'm finding freedom right now.

I'm really not an expert at running a law office. Far from it. Nevertheless, I know a thing or two about transitioning to solo practice. I made the transition; and my finances are thriving, my family is thriving, and my client relationships are thriving. I think my dogs even like me better.

I'm never going to overstate my skill in all of this. I stumbled into a lot of this success. However, luck comes to those who simply keep moving forward. You can't stumble into anything, good or bad, if you're sitting in one spot, watching life happen to you like you're a spectator. So even though I can't come to you as the mastermind who created the perfect plan to go solo ahead of time, I can look back on what I did (intentionally or otherwise) and tell you what worked and what didn't. Whether I planned my success or got lucky doesn't really matter; hindsight is 20/20, so let's use my hindsight looking back on a successful transition to solo practice, and use it to your advantage.

One of the mistakes I made was waiting way too long. Going solo wasn't even a long-term goal of mine, to be honest. I fought the urge to go solo for decades. I thought about it from time to time. I even had this fantasy about ramping up a business that did nothing but state annual reports for clients every year. I thought about going out on my own with partners. I thought about leaving the practice of law completely and just going back into sales. I thought about leaving capitalism entirely and becoming a pastor.[1] I thought about a lot of things, but it was all just daydreaming. For years, it was never anything other than a mental exercise while I limped along in jammed traffic on the way to the office, but there comes a day when some of us realize that employment is not an option anymore. That can either be a tough day or a liberating day. Or both.

I wanted to write this book because I spent almost all of my life as an employee with the overwhelming feeling that I was a disappointment to those around me. And I hated it. It had a profound effect on me. I got to a point where I believed I genuinely was inadequate, that I just couldn't do my job. If you had asked me five years ago if I was qualified to write a book about anything, I would have laughed. I was barely scraping by at work.

---

[1] This one stings a little, actually, because I was offered a free ride to seminary and passed on it. That was dumb. So one mistake you can learn from is that you shouldn't walk away from something you genuinely believe to be a calling. Nevertheless, there's still time for me on this one. We'll see.

I'll talk a lot about my flaws in this book. I'm hard on myself. Most people who go solo are that way. But as much as I like talking about my flaws, I should clarify that I'm wasn't a total disaster as an employee. Some things always went well; they were just balanced out by my struggles. Still, I had my consistent victories. Mainly, I have always done well when it came to sales. I received my first real sales training from a company called Primerica. It's a multilevel marketing company that sells life insurance and mutual funds. The idea is that you sell some financial products and make a little bit of money on that, but where you get the big money is building a team below you, hence the "multilevel" aspect of the marketing. The org chart looks a little like a (let's be honest) pyramid. Please don't sue me, Primerica.

The key at Primerica was recruiting, but I was thriving on the selling. I didn't really like the recruiting and team building. I tried it. It wasn't great. However, I loved sitting at a kitchen table with a family and selling them products I knew they needed. I loved watching their reaction as I dramatically lowered their costs and helped them implement a real plan to retire with money in their pockets and no debt. For most of these people, retirement was a distant dream that seemed impossible. I helped them change that, and I loved doing it, but I didn't like the recruiting, and the main path to success at Primerica is building a team. No, thanks.

I would have assumed that I would be the type of person who was great at building a team. I like meeting new people. I like inspiring people. I've actually had a good amount of success motivating groups of people to accomplish projects for church. But it never clicks for me in an employment setting. Something about it just doesn't work. It's just not one of my gifts, and doing it quickly sucks the joy out of anything I'm working on. So I moved on from Primerica after a couple of years.

Aside from the team building, which I didn't like, the sales training at Primerica was excellent. This organization is a place that most people don't list on their resume because it was a weird multilevel marketing thing they tried for a while. Few make a career out of it. However, the sales training at Primerica is fully legit. They taught me the keys that I'll teach you later in this book. The main lesson being that sales is about connecting people's needs to the products that satisfy those needs. Connecting. Nothing more. It's not about twisting arms to get people to buy something they don't want. And ever since going through that training, sales has come naturally to me.

As naturally as sales came, I've always struggled when it came to productivity. My sales skills made it easy to get a job because an interview is little more than a sales pitch. I'm good at interviewing. The saying is that people hire people who are like themselves, and I'm good at mirroring and all of the other sales techniques out there that help you nail an interview. So interviews are always fine for me. I've actually only gone on one interview that didn't result in a job offer. Sales (and interviewing) comes naturally to me. But things became difficult after getting that job offer. At some point, it doesn't matter how much an employer likes you. They are going to show you your office, introduce you to your support staff, hand you a laptop and expect you to perform well at your job. They're going to expect you to produce good work product. And lots of it.

None of my employers were slave drivers. I didn't leave jobs because my employers drove me to bill ridiculous numbers of hours. Lots of firms do that, but not the ones where I worked; it was quite the opposite. The annual hour requirements were actually fairly low, and that actually made things worse for me and made my issues with productivity so frustrating.

It's easy to complain about blowing it at work when your employer is asking for ten billable hours a day. That's insane. My employers wanted somewhere around half of that. And I still wasn't hitting the mark. Even worse than that, my employers actually did quite a lot to try to help me with my productivity. Much to my dismay then, I had no one else to blame. I fell short of their very reasonable expectations or, at best, hung on by a thread. I hated this daily struggle with failure where everyone else seemed to be doing just fine, but as it turns out, my productivity wasn't quite as bad as I thought. I'll go into more detail on that later. But it was an issue, nonetheless.

Quick summary: I'm good at sales and bad at productivity. Does that somehow make me special? At this point, you may be wondering if you've wasted whatever you spent to buy this book. I'm far from perfect, and reading about my shortcomings and what I did with them may be the most important aspect of this book. I'm pointing out my flaws to make it clear that going solo is not reserved for the elite among us. I'm not elite. I'm barely average. In theory, if I was writing a typical book about going solo, the opening pages should be about how amazing I am. I should be trying to convince you that I am the guru of going solo because I'm incredibly talented, and if you read these pages, you can be just as amazing as I am. Instead, I'm telling you that I struggled to do even the most basic tasks of my job. Why would I do that? Because I'm trying to convince you of the single most important aspect of succeeding as a solo: you don't need to be a master of anything to go solo and thrive.

I need to dispel the misconception that people go solo because they are exceptionally gifted. Solo practice is more like the island of misfit toys than anything else. But there is a way for even the most misfit toy to craft his or her life into something compellingly rewarding. That's what I've accomplished; I've found success and freedom *despite* my struggles, not by eliminating them. Trust me, I tried.

So that's why I'm writing this book. And I'll take plenty of digs at myself along the way to prove to you that the shortcomings you obsess over about yourself are not the roadblocks that you think they are; they might even be your strongest tools for success. When I first went solo, I was simply hoping that all my shortcomings didn't immediately sink the ship. As it turns out, they've become my greatest assets. They were simply assets that didn't work well in a traditional employment setting. In a solo environment, things started clicking in a way they never had before, even with my flaws.

If you're sitting at home after a hard day and thinking you probably can't hack it on your own, you are exactly where I was five years ago. However, over time, I started thinking I might not be as inadequate as I was feeling; I started wondering if I was really the problem at all. Maybe my job was the problem. In my mind, this initially meant my *employer* was the problem. So to solve that problem, I changed jobs. Problem solved? I thought so. This new employer brought me in as a partner. I had respect, which I felt was missing in my prior job. They gave me quite a bit of freedom that was missing in my prior job, and these were (and are) genuinely good people. But still, productivity issues lingered. There was a honeymoon period where I was killing it on productivity, but that honeymoon period faded. Productivity dropped to the low levels it had hit before and even worse now that I had more freedom and no one looking over my shoulder every minute of the day.

Perhaps my employers were not the problem, then. At some point, the only common denominator of all of these *bad* employers was me. Am I the problem? Or is my employer the problem? Ultimately, the answer was…both. I wasn't right for my employers, and they weren't right for me. Neither one of us was, in any overwhelming way, wrong, but both of us were wrong for each other. But even though I was wrong for my employer, I was right for my clients.

What about you? Are you wrong for your employer but right for your clients? Is it possible that you could enjoy greater success than you ever have if you just did it on your own, playing by your own rules, living by your own standards, truly having the freedom to be the person who your clients love but your employers can barely tolerate?

Since going solo, I've done well financially, which is the number one concern for people wishing they could go solo. I stepped out on my own and generated just under $400,000 in revenue in my first full year. Not billing but actual cash in the door. That number sounds amazing, and it even took me by surprise when I heard it during a meeting with my CPA. It's a good number. But it doesn't all stay in your pocket. One of the easiest mistakes to make as a solo is to pursue the same amount of money you made as an employee. Don't do that. There are a lot of people reaching into your pockets when you go solo, so your revenue goal probably needs to be a lot higher than you're thinking. More on that later.

So I produced this good amount of revenue, and I did it from my living room with a laptop and a laser printer. That's great. Let's take this success, mix it in with my impressive list of shortcomings, and use it all to figure out how to build *your* solo lifestyle from the ground up. Your solo story won't be the same as mine. I'm a walking textbook of screwups and victories and proof that success as a solo is within reach of literally anyone. Let's get you out on your own while repeating my wins and avoiding my losses.

This chapter makes going solo sound simple, so why doesn't everyone go solo? And why do some solos struggle? I've spoken to enough people to know that many solo practitioners, whether in law or elsewhere, are genuinely struggling. They are thrilled if they can just cover the mortgage payment at home. Their spouse works because they have to, not because they want to; and to generate this scraping by level of income, they are still working nonstop. But I don't think they need to. Let's start there.

Why do so many solos struggle on their own while a handful of them really knock it out of the park? And how do we ensure that you end up in the second category? Let's begin your journey toward solo life by diagnosing the difference between struggling and thriving as a solo.

BROKE LAWYERS? YES, IT'S A THING

Every lawyer is swimming in cash with a huge house and a fancy sports car. Right? Not exactly. There are two schools of attorneys: those who work in a law firm and those who work on their own. As you've read already, for some people (spoiler alert, me), working in a law firm is not the solution. Well, that shouldn't be a big deal, right? Just go solo and get crazy rich. No problem. Right?

Wrong. Most attorneys really struggle when they go solo. Many end up back at law firms or end up struggling to make ends meet. They struggle to bring their clients with them. They struggle to generate new business once they are on their own. They struggle to find the right staff to help them. They struggle with collections. They struggle with productivity. Overall…they struggle.

But there are also some solo attorneys who genuinely thrive on their own. The primary purpose of this book is to figure out what the thriving solo attorneys did that is different than those who struggle. How did they build their client base? How did they take those clients with them when they went solo? How did they continue to attract new business once they were on their own? How did they serve clients with varying needs while only having a specific skillset?

In 2018, myshingle.com[2] posted a good article on the disparity of solo attorney incomes. The article cited IRS data showing average solo attorneys' income of $50,000 a year. With an income like that, it's going to be hard to keep you reading this book. Solos were

---

[2] https://myshingle.com/2018/05/articles/future-trends/solo-small-firm -lawyers-average-198k-year/.

billing as little as two hours per day. That hurts. On the other hand, other studies were showing solos earning between $140,000 and $226,000, and there were outliers earning far more than that. There must be a lesson to be taken from those who went solo and knocked it out of the park.

There are only a minority of solos who are doing so well. Most, about two-thirds, are just barely paying the bills. Let's solve that problem and open the door for everyone to enjoy the freedom that comes with being a solo attorney but without sacrificing the income that most assume can only be achieved at a large firm.

As part of my research for this book, I read a lot of articles and opinion pieces about solo attorneys, and I was surprised to find many articles essentially saying, "Solo attorneys may not be the losers we all thought they were." Really? I never actually thought that solo attorneys were losers. I was always a bit jealous, actually, but it is interesting that there are at least a decent number of people out there that see solos as losers. No doubt the income struggles that most solos have would be part of that equation, but there is also a perception that solos went solo because they just couldn't hack it in a law firm. Well, if you read the introduction, you know that the prior sentence is actually true about me. It's literally the subtitle of this book. But I didn't go solo because I was failing so badly at providing legal services—my clients love working with me. It was more that the way I was working wasn't conducive to a law firm structure. My success skyrocketed after I went solo. I earned more in my second full month as a solo than I had ever earned in any month as an employee of a law firm. So perhaps the traditional law firm structure just isn't the solution for everyone. Perhaps the traditional law firm structure is actually holding some people back.

One of the phenomena I observed while still employed was that solo attorneys often eventually look for work at law firms. This proves the theory! Solo attorneys eventually must come begging for work again with their tail tucked between their legs, admitting that they can't hack it on their own without a law firm environment.

When I was working at a law firm, we had a solo immigration attorney join the firm. It must be because he failed in his solo practice, right? But then, something striking happened. He quit after about six months and went back to solo life. This wasn't the only time this happened. Similarly, a solo residential real estate attorney joined the firm and went back out on his own about a year later. Then another solo attorney came to interview at that same firm and took a hard pass on a chance at employment with a fast-growing firm. Today, he's still solo and thriving.

If joining a firm was confirmation that going solo was a mistake, then why were these attorneys returning to solo life after such a short period of time? What was really going on here?

In writing this book, I talked to each of these attorneys and several others and learned that their reasons for wanting to join a firm were precisely the opposite of failure. They were, in fact, generating so much business on their own that they thought they would be able to increase their income by bringing in a ton of work while still working their own files and then farming out the rest of it to other attorneys in the firm and earning a huge referral bonus (we don't call them commissions in the legal industry because we're *very sophisticated* people. Pinkies out, everyone).

But this obviously fell apart and did so fairly quickly. The dream of farming out all of this work to other attorneys and earning big bonuses didn't really pan out. That type of structure can definitely be lucrative, but it's a lot to manage. You're spending a lot of time managing other people, training them to handle these projects the way you like them handled, and this starts to cut into the time you're dedicating to your clients, and clients don't like it. The joy of practicing law and serving your clients becomes an endless string of meetings, interoffice e-mails, committees, and pretty much every other thing that a solo simply never needs to do. Even assuming the increase in income were to happen (which it didn't for most of these solos who got jobs), it comes at a hefty price. And the largest price paid was the loss of freedom.

People inclined to go solo don't like start times and end times where you're expected to be in the office. We don't like dress codes. I actually dress nicer now than I did when I worked at a law firm, and I'm sitting in my former living room every day. I'm doing it because

I want to, not because I got a memo about not wearing flip-flops, except on every other Friday. Solos don't like being told what to do. We're the ones fidgeting our way through meetings, waiting desperately for them to be over. We're the ones anxious to get back on the phone with clients and out-of-the-office kitchen, where the gossip is flying.

So it turns out that these solos, at least, aren't losers at all. In fact, they are generating more business than they can handle and thought (for a while) that joining a firm was the solution. In reality, these solos are killing it. Let's look at what they are doing and contrast it to the solos out there who are struggling just to make ends meet. There are some definite patterns. First, the most successful solos are specialists and not generalist. Second, the top solos are rainmakers. They are great at sales.

Before you go into panic mode because you are neither of these things, remember the main theme of this book. You are not going to sit around, waiting to magically become a specialist and a rainmaker; you are literally going to turn yourself into both of these things *while you're still employed.* And when the time is right, you'll strike out on your own. Don't worry about it if you're not where you need to be on these points right now; you'll get there. And you'll do so well in advance of going solo.

Critical Key Number One: Top Earning Solo Attorneys Are Not Generalists

The top earners specialize. One solo I know does extremely well, and his only area of practice is ERISA litigation. He doesn't draft ERISA plans. He doesn't go to court for any other reason than an ERISA case. He doesn't do real estate closings or form corporations. He would have to hire another lawyer to review his office lease. Literally the only thing he does is go to court on ERISA cases. That's hyperfocused, and he's good at it.

What about other practice groups? Residential real estate closings are one of the hardest ways to make decent money as an attorney. When I was with a law firm, we called it the black hole of billing.

It was just accepted that residential real estate closings were a loss leader. But I know solo attorneys doing only closings and absolutely killing it. Because it's literally the *only thing they do*.

The desire to try to help every potential client you might meet is natural. But it's also a recipe for that $50,000 average solo income that you have to work yourself to death to earn. The cliché "Jack of all trades, master of none" is a cliché for a reason. If you're peddling whatever service someone might need, then you're marketing yourself as a commodity, and the problem with commodities is that people don't like paying for them, and they are easy to replace. Consider the movies where you see guys in suits yelling and screaming on a trading floor and flashing crazy hand signals, trying to either buy or sell stocks or commodities. What is the one rule on that floor? They don't care who they get them from; they care about the price. Whoever meets the price they want gets the sale. It's as simple as that.

This is how most solo attorneys practice law. They launch their solo firm and head out into the world, screaming that they offer literally any service a person could want and assuring the public that they'll do it cheaper than anyone. And they are treated just like the guys on the trading floor. There will always be someone offering your commodity at a cheaper price, and when they do, you're pushed to the side. By trying to be all things to all people, you're setting yourself up for a miserable existence of competing with online do-it-yourself legal platforms and every cut-rate attorney in your area who is willing to bill at half of what you're worth, and you're almost never going to form long-term relationships with your clients. It's a nightmare that you can entirely avoid. But as discussed in the previous chapter, you don't walk out on your own and then start specializing. You specialize first while still employed and then take that focused skill set out on your own once it's been perfected and fully developed.

Specializing gives you the power to develop the kind of relationships with clients that make you love coming to the office ever day (or living room, as the case may be). It allows you to charge what you're actually worth and to work with clients who have a genuine need for that specialized knowledge and don't complain about paying for it.

Specializing solves a lot of problems. Get started now on identifying the area you'd like to specialize in, and just dive in. It takes time, and don't be surprised if your direction changes a lot over time. It never crossed my mind that I would be helping clients develop, build, license, and manage senior housing projects when I was at a firm. But that's more than half of my business now. I specialized in pure transactional work, and that took me down a path that was unexpected but not entirely out of left field. Be ready to follow your path where it takes you.

Doing this involves some risk. What if you temporarily chase a rabbit hole that ends up going nowhere? It's okay. You're doing it before quitting your job, so that risk is substantially mitigated, and you'll have work being fed to you from your firm, so you won't be sitting there twiddling your thumbs while you wait for your specialized field to take off.

Do the work the firm gives you, and do it well. Be great at that, and work hard at it. They're paying you after all. But at the same time, work to develop your own specialization. It will slowly grow to a point where you're having to turn away work from the firm to complete the specialized work you're bringing in on your own.

I know I keep saying this, but it's worth repeating. Like everything else in this book, you're going to do all of this long before you ever go solo, and you'll just continue with that success once you're out on your own as opposed to just getting started with specialization after you've walked away from a steady salary.

Critical Key Number Two: Top Earning Solo Attorneys Are Rainmakers

Top earning solo attorneys are great at generating business. It probably even looks like they do it naturally without even trying. Generating business consists of a few key elements: they know how to bring in new clients, they know how to develop strong and long-lasting bonds with their clients (their clients would follow them literally anywhere), and most often (depending on practice type), they have a *consistent* stream of new business without a lot of peaks and valleys. And what I can tell you with certainty is that that none of these traits comes to them naturally. These traits have been developed over a long period of time through an endless series of trial and error attempts. They might have gone through those trial an error attempts without knowing it, but they definitely went through them.

One of the things I loved about the first law firm I worked for was the founder's willingness to try different things. He handed out books for all of the attorneys to read. One was on guerilla marketing techniques. This book blew the doors off traditional direct mail marketing and presented strategies for highly aggressive and totally out of the box marketing initiatives. We tried a bunch of them. It was fun. But in the end, it didn't generate a ton of business. So we moved on. But we moved on without ever regretting having tried; it was a learning process. And despite not being as successful as we had hoped, that exercise did affect our marketing angles going forward at least to some degree.

This is how he always operated. He was constantly learning, constantly trying new things, capitalizing on every success, and learning from every failure. People around him would most definitely call him a natural rainmaker. "He doesn't even have to try. Clients just flock to him." In fairness, he should be offended by this. His "natural" ability to bring in clients was more like a nonstop self-education regimen on perfecting the art of running a law firm. It's like saying an Olympic athlete is just a natural runner and completely missing the hours in training she spent every day for years on end. The funniest phrase I've heard on this was from Pat Flynn, a very successful internet marketer, who said, "It took me fifteen years of day and night work to become an overnight success."

So yes, to a certain extent, successful solos are natural rainmakers. But they weren't born that way; they made themselves into natural rainmakers. There is a chapter on this topic to provide you some guidance on doing exactly the same thing for yourself without changing who you are naturally wired up to be, and you're going to do so before you ever write a resignation letter. You're not going to read up on how to become a rainmaker after you go solo; you're going to turn yourself into a rainmaker while you still have a job and then ride that momentum into your journey of going solo.

Living the Dream

One moment that sticks out in my memory was a bit funny. I was handling a residential real estate closing, and the wire transfer to fund the closing was running behind schedule. The opposing attorney, buyer, seller, and I were all sitting around the closing table, making small talk while we waited; and the opposing attorney was a solo. Somehow the conversation turned to the upcoming wedding season and the number of weddings this attorney had been invited to recently. He commented, "I like celebrating a wedding as much as the next guy, but after a while, it's expensive. Every one of these weddings is a $700 or $800 wedding gift, and then there's the travelling. It's a lot."

Well, we all had a good time giving him a bit of ribbing about his extraordinary wedding gift budget and politely asking if he might be willing to adopt us into his very giving family. Seven hundred dollars for a wedding gift? Just how much income was this guy earning on his own? This was one of those moments that had me really thinking about going out on my own. This guy had what he described as a small practice. He had only one support staff, drove a nice car, and, at the very least, seemed to have a healthy budget for wedding gifts. Why wouldn't everyone want to enjoy this level of success? The initial seeds were planted; I was starting to think I could pull off going solo someday.

The things that this attorney discovered were the same things that started to bother me over time and caused me to strike out on my own. The main missing ingredient was freedom. This attorney had come to love the freedom of running a business however he liked. He had no committees to answer to, no billable hour requirements to meet, and no facetime requirements in the office.

I considered his financial situation too. If you know how to bring in business, it's almost impossible to make as much money working at a law firm compared to what you can make on your own. When you are on your own, you have all the risk. I get that. But you also have all of the revenue. That's a compelling reason to consider going solo. Let's not oversimplify the benefit of keeping all of your revenue. That "keeping all the revenue" dream turns into a nightmare if there isn't *enough* revenue, and for many solo attorneys, that's the problem.

I recently did some research on solo attorney incomes and was surprised to find that the average income of solo attorneys is far less than $100,000 per year. You can easily make that much working at a law firm, so I can see why people might be a bit worried about breaking out on their own. But in my continued research, I found that this average is quite misleading. There are a lot of solo attorneys doing very well, earning at least $200,000 per year and often well over $300,000. If that's true, why is the average way down at $100,000? It turns out that most solo attorneys are just dabbling at going solo and are spending about as much time looking for a job at a firm as they are building their own practice. They never dive in headfirst. They are forever hedging their bets, and as a result, they never find the job they really want and never find the success as a solo that they really want. They're in a form of professional purgatory where they are working their fingers to the bone and accomplishing neither of their objectives.

These semi-committed solo attorneys are dragging down the average considerably. They are living on, perhaps, a few thousand dollars a month, in sharp contrast to the solo, earning a few thousand dollars a week or over a couple thousand dollars a day. They are still trying to work the way they worked at a law firm and waiting for it to kick in and start paying off. It never will. They never really embrace the ability to define themselves on their own terms, and they just don't thrive the way I really wish they could. Being a solo attorney is entirely different than working at a law firm. Working like you're at a firm while being solo is like trying to jam a square peg into a round hole.

Freedom isn't just a benefit of going solo; it's a requirement. You need to define yourself and truly be yourself because *you are the product*, and that product is the only thing this business has to offer. It's funny. I've been doing this for a while now, but I still slip into the old habits. I've recently had a lot of work coming in, and I wasn't happy. My clients weren't happy. My health was slipping a bit. I was working all the time. And my wife said to me, "You're working like you used to work at the firm, and it's not working." She had asked me to go on a walk with her in the middle of the day. The middle of the day! Was she nuts? I've got work to do! But, as always, she was right. I shut off the computer and went on a nice walk with her. I worked a little later than I usually do to get the projects done for the day.

At her suggestion, I recaptured the freedom I originally wanted when I went solo in the first place, and my work product improved. My delivery time improved (even though I was taking more time to *be me*), and my clients were happier. As soon as I started acting like a law firm, I started getting law firm results: irritated clients, irritated spouse, and irritated kids.

This space of trying to act like a real law firm is something of a professional purgatory. Helping dig out of this purgatory, or preferably avoiding it in the first place, is my mission. How can we avoid this lifestyle? How can we avoid jumping from the frying pan of law firm life to the fire of uninspired solo life? How do we get to a point where we make the plunge into going solo without ever looking back with no backup plan? The key is actually very simple. Of course, you're going to be timid in your solo journey if you just dove into it without any foundation beneath you. I'd be timid too. When going solo, you don't just wake up one day and walk out on your job; you plan it. And you plan it for a very long time. Probably much longer than you might think. You also remove all guesswork of success by perfecting all the skills you need as a solo while you are still an employee. And by the time to walk into your boss's office to hand in your resignation letter, you're going to know that you're ready, and you're going to know that you can support yourself on your own.

You can never remove *all* risk, but you can sure as heck remove a lot of the risk and develop the confidence you need to be on your own long before you quit your job.

There are the two fundamental keys to this entire book. First, plan ahead (way ahead). Second, test and perfect your solo skills while you still have a job. It's really that simple. These two concepts are the foundation of setting yourself up to enjoy the income, freedom, and the happiness that I've been able to find as a solo attorney.

And I've done it all without any superhero skills. One of the things you'll learn about me is that I'm an exceptionally flawed person. This wasn't an impediment to going solo; these flaws are what made going solo an absolute necessity for me. So let's start by finding out if there is something inside you that has you burning to go out on your own the same way I did.

REVERSE SCALE

Bigger Isn't Better

Going solo isn't only about the benefits you receive. I have worked at medium sized firms and gone against the biggest firms in the country, and I've seen their limitations. Yes, I have realized life-changing benefits from going solo, but I also believe that I'm delivering better services to my clients than ever before. I don't suggest that going solo is the only way to practice law, but I do suggest that solo law firms fill a need in the marketplace that is growing rapidly.

Solo firms are solving a lot of the problems that are inherent to larger operations, and technology has created an opportunity that has never existed before. The assumption that you only get top quality legal services from medium or large law firms is being turned on its head by solo attorneys who are doing great work at a fraction of the cost of larger firms, and they are doing this at a higher personal income than they could ever earn at a traditional firm.

What drove me away from the comfort of a steady paycheck? In addition to the struggles I've described already, it was also the constant nagging feeling that I was surrounded, for lack of a better term, by more than I needed to be. Legal services are shockingly expensive and not because your providers have had to invest in expensive machinery like an auto manufacturer; it's expensive simply because the providers themselves like to be well-compensated (me included), but they also surround themselves with a lot of necessities that aren't necessary. The bigger the firm, the bigger the expenditures on these unnecessary things.

If you've ever seen *Shark Tank*, you've probably heard an enthusiastic budding entrepreneur tell the sharks, "With this investment, we'll be able to scale the business and drive down costs." Most people know that if you order a thousand widgets, they are expensive; but if you order a hundred thousand widgets, the per unit price drops. We see this in our daily lives. WalMart prices are low because they order a shipping container full of products instead of a box full. The larger the operation, the more these economies of scale drive down your per unit costs. Large corporations are absolute masters at it. When you scale, your prices go down, and your volume goes up, unless you're a law firm.

Look at the average law firm. As a law firm grows larger, we see the exact opposite effect take place. Prices don't go down; they go up. Hourly rates at larger firms are higher, sometimes dramatically higher than those charged by solo attorneys. As opposed to seeing the economies of scale driving prices down (the way we see with WalMart and McDonalds), we see prices rise dramatically the bigger you get. This bothered me while I was working at law firms.

In one firm, I started as their eighth attorney. When I left, they were at twenty-five. During that time, we went from a building that had literally been a warehouse for a swimming pool maintenance company to a very nice office on the seventh floor of a beautiful office building located right in the middle of a thriving business community. The new office was wonderful, and my oversized office furnishings barely made a dent in the gymnasium-size office I was given, and I wasn't even a top performing attorney. My office was great, but by comparison to some others, it was average. I had a great view out huge windows and sat at a giant desk with my secretary right outside the door. It was great. It was expensive. And the people paying for it all were the clients I was serving. I felt surrounded by expenses that were not irresponsible or even excessive, but they were simply nonessential and didn't truly need to be passed on to our clients. We could have practiced law just as well without them. Some would disagree, but that's how I felt.

Being honest (as much as I say I didn't like the nonessentials), walking away from this environment was difficult. We had an entire conference room set up strictly for Kanban boards (a popular project management system that this firm had absolutely mastered). A large kitchen, a beautiful reception area, everything you would want for your thriving and growing law practice. But at what cost? While one part of me was looking around, loving my new digs, part of me was seeing overhead everywhere. Rent, secretaries, accounting staff, buildout cost, truckloads of new furniture. This was an expensive move, an expensive buildout, and a fairly expensive office.

Don't get me wrong. This was not a ridiculous overspend. It was a nice office, but it wasn't excessive. We didn't have $50,000 paintings on the wall and fine Corinthian leather sofas in the partners' offices. That's why I say this was strictly my issue. The classic "it's not you, it's me" scenario. Even though, by traditional standards, the office was not overdone, it was costly; and in my own mind, I saw it as excessive. Perhaps *excessive* is not the right word; *unnecessary* would be more accurate. I can see why someone would like to work there, but it all seemed like it wasn't really needed. We hardly ever met with clients in the office anyway. We basically built this new office for ourselves.

There is nothing wrong with having a nice office. I assume that even low-cost leader WalMart probably has a nice executive office complex, but that nice executive office complex was built upon the foundation of lowering prices for customers. This new law office was built upon a foundation that saw hourly rates go up as time went by as opposed to going down. Every year, more attorneys were added; and every year, each lawyer's hourly rate went up. We were costing clients more every year while delivering the same services. Something about it didn't sit well with me. However, this is perfectly standard within the industry. Clients never complained. I didn't leave the comfort of a law firm partnership because clients were expressing a backlash against the office decor; this was an entirely personal issue for me. I looked around and saw significant expenses that were not critical to the delivery of quality legal services. I sat in my office, contemplating the fact that it had been weeks, or possibly months, since I had actually met a client in our office. The business of law was changing, and clients were signing up over the phone or via video conference. The question of whether an office was needed at all began to creep into my mind.

This thought magnified as I switched firms to one in downtown Chicago. Again, nicely decorated but nothing over the top. We were on the twenty-second floor of a building right on the Chicago River with great views. My office at this new firm was quite a bit smaller but still very nice; and I could watch boaters, barges, and water taxis drift down the river while I ate lunch at my desk. What struck me at this office was storage space. This firm had at least thirty years of files on shelves in two very large storage rooms. This was, in my mind, an extraordinary amount of financial investment just to store sheets of paper.

Every square foot of office space, every staff salary, every painting on the wall, every giant copy machine, the computer system, the phone system. All of it. Every single dollar spent on these items was a dollar that didn't directly contribute to the practice of law, and that doesn't even begin to address the largest "expense" (if you want to call it that) which was to provide a profit to the partners of the firm. Of course there is nothing wrong with the partners earning a profit, but that profit distribution, whatever it is, does not directly contribute to the delivery of legal services. What the partners paid me (assuming I'm not overpaid) was the direct cost of providing legal services, and there isn't much more than that. Most of my surroundings were unnecessary overhead in my not-so-humble opinion.

I started thinking about a UPS truck. The United Parcel Service knocks it out of the park when it comes to efficiency. Their delivery trucks are perfectly suited to the task at hand. The trucks perfectly define the concept of a purpose-built vehicle. The vehicle does its job and has nothing extra built into it, but at the same time, it's built well. UPS doesn't cheap out when it comes to the engine and reliability. The components that are built into the truck are built well. There simply aren't any extra components. No one would think it excessive if UPS simply purchased a fleet of the popular Sprinter-style work vans. However, these vans have stuff that UPS doesn't really need built into a delivery truck, so they started with a blank sheet of paper and designed a truck that does the bare minimum but does it really well.

That was my concept when I started to design my own office. I need a desk, a place to work, a chair, a computer, a printer and scanner, a phone, a secure e-mail system, a billing system, and, well… that's about it. When I stripped down my day-to-day activities and really examined the minimum viable setup that I needed to deliver legal services to my clients, I was surprised at how little I needed. (Okay, I admit I splurged on the chair. I bought one of those swanky big tufted leather lawyer chairs, but it was used so whatever.) I could function exactly the way I was functioning at a law firm in downtown Chicago from my living room with a bare minimum of technology and equipment. Everything else that surrounded me in my nice downtown office was tantamount to pulling extra dollars out of my clients' pockets and spending it on things that literally didn't need to exist at all for my type of clients.

I ran the numbers, and I could significantly increase my personal income while also significantly decreasing my clients' costs; or, when said another way, I could drop my hourly rate, save my clients thousands of dollars, and double my personal income.

So I went to Best Buy, bought a laptop, a printer/scanner, and a desk lamp. I bought a used desk and dragged a large cabinet we weren't using up from the basement. I ordered business cards, letterhead, and envelopes. A friend from church designed a great logo that I still use today. Almost two years into this experience and I'm still working from the original box of letterhead. I bought MS Office and signed up for a Cloud-based billing system. I even made my own website on WordPress. I splurged and got the $18 per year option with no ads. I'm still using it today even though it's obviously a DIY job, but it gets the job done. Then, I walked into my managing partner's office and let him know that I was going out on my own. It was really that simple.

This solution is right for me. And based on how well business is going, it's right for a lot of my clients. At first, I was very nervous about working from home and the stigma that it carries. I was worried I'd look like a rookie or just generally unprofessional. But almost two years into this, I now celebrate my humble surroundings. When clients ask, "Do you work out of your house?" I proudly shoot back, "Definitely. I have a meeting space I can use for clients who need it, but 99 percent of the time, I'm working out of what used to be my living room." I don't hide it, and I don't call myself Voigt and Associates. There are no associates, and I love that. I love being honest and upfront about what used to give me anxiety. On my website, there is a page titled "Small by Design," celebrating the smallness of my firm.

The number of clients I've lost because I lack a *real* office? Zero, as far as I know. I suppose it's possible that people looked me up online and saw a house instead of an office building and decided not to call. I'm not planning to do any market research to find out. For the market that I'm serving, the clients I truly enjoy working with don't care. They don't want to drive downtown to meet me in person anyway. Most of the time, they are relieved that they don't need to do so. Even beyond that, I'm finding that many of the clients I thought were working out of traditional offices are, themselves, working from home. One of my clients has more than a thousand employees, operates around twenty buildings, and has no office. Their street address is a UPS Store. Times have changed, and the absolute necessity of a traditional office has, for my market, almost entirely disappeared.

This doesn't render the traditional law firm completely useless. I just personally don't need it. That's me. The concept of a law firm is not suddenly outdated just because I personally don't get much benefit from it. Law firms still serve a valuable purpose for certain types of lawyers and certain types of clients. Heck, maybe even the vast majority of lawyers and clients benefit from a traditional law firm structure. I just knew, looking at my own clients and my own work style, that I didn't need it. I rarely met with my clients. Even when I had a nice office, I usually travelled to client offices to meet them there anyway. I spoke to most of my clients via my personal cell phone. Whenever I was sick, working from home was entirely seamless. Clients never even knew I was e-mailing them from my house.

The reality of my ability to utilize even the most basic modern technology to run a fully functional law firm became very clear to me. I walked out of a $170,000-a-year job with a great view of the Chicago River and set up shop in what used to be my living room. And I'm far enough into it today to report that it's all working without the huge monthly rent, the fancy paintings on the wall, the giant copiers, and the giant rooms to store paper files. For my type of client and my type of work habits, this works. My clients are happier. Their legal costs are down. My wife and kids are happier. I'm definitely happier. And I have the freedom to work the way I've always wanted to work.

I had an interesting moment the other day. My wife and I met a client for lunch, and he's known me for a long time. He was with me at my first firm and my second, and we had gotten to know each other well over the years. We were having the normal client lunch with good conversation and getting caught up on family and business. He stopped mid-sentence at one point and said, "I don't want to speak out of turn, but I have to say something. You look happy. Really happy. I've never seen you like this. It's great to see." It caused me to stop and reflect on where I had been and how far I'd come. While I like that I've increased my personal income, what I love the most is that my life is genuinely better. I'm *more me*, whatever that means, and apparently it shows. That was a good lunch. It's one of those moments that will stay with me for a long time.

Having seen the upside-down scaling effect of increasing costs as firm size went up, I simply couldn't unsee it. And I knew that there was a more efficient, a more stripped down, and a much simpler way to meet the needs of my particular clients by casting off all of the dollars that law firms spend. I have a nice office with nice equipment. Like the UPS truck, I didn't save money by purchasing cheap equipment; I saved money by buying only what I needed. Top quality but no fluff.

The question of whether this smaller business model works is what plagues people struggling with the desire to go out on their own. It's easy to write about a theory of the reverse scaling of large service firms, but if you're going to quit your job, you don't need catchy phrases. You need income. Will this small-by-design lifestyle actually produce results that pay the mortgage? In a word, yes. The smaller I get, the lower my clients' cost and the higher my profit margin, and that's even after slashing my hourly rate. That's the exact opposite of the scaling that everyone on *Shark Tank* is trying to achieve. I strongly believe that in the professional services industry, reverse scaling works. Smaller is better.

I've lowered my billable rate by about $50 per hour, and my clients like the savings. I also dropped my flat fee for annual compliance work by about half the rates my former firm was charging. At first, my personal income shot up considerably, from a gross salary of $170,000 to about $240,000. Bear in mind that this isn't all profit. I have expenses such as monthly software costs, insurance, office supplies, and so on. All in, I would estimate that I was running at the equivalent of a $200,000 gross salary right out of the gate when I went out on my own. Not bad.

I had a funny phone call a few weeks ago with a former law school classmate. He was a third year student (called a 3L in law school) when I was a fresh first year or 1L. I believe he went out on his own right out of law school, which makes him something of a badass in my world. He called with a question about an attorney I used to work with. He was curious about her litigation style, etc. As it always does, the conversation turned to how business is going, and he was curious how I was doing on my own. He cautioned me to be patient because it takes a few years to get the income back up to what it was when I was traditionally employed. It was a little bit awkward, but I told him that I had actually made substantially more in my first month on my own than I had the month before at my regular job. He responded that it's important to be careful about the occasional good month because there will always be a bad month. And it was a little awkward again, but I told him that I'd made more every month since then. I've never had a down month. His response was funny. "Oh. Um, okay. Wow. Well that's great."

That short conversation is the true motivation for this book. The life of a solo attorney doesn't have to be a stress-filled struggle to pay your bills all while praying to your higher power that this doesn't all blow up in your face without warning. This can be a good life, and the pitfalls can be avoided. That's not a pipe dream; it's my daily reality. And I want it to be yours.

I originally set a goal of billing $20,000 a month, but I quickly increased that to a goal of $34,000 per month. That monthly amount became a bit stressful and pushed me to work after dinner away from my family, so I recently scaled it back to $30,000 per month. I think I have found my sweet spot. Time will tell, and my calculation of my monthly goal is anything but scientific. I had raised the goal from $20,000 to $30,000 per month after about half a year. And then I had to file my taxes. Ouch! So I tacked on another $4,000 to the goal each month to buffer the blow of self-employment tax. After doing that for a while, I came to the somewhat funny realization that $30,000 is still quite an income, and that I could get by just fine even with the surprisingly high burden of self-employment tax.

I've been running at that goal since then. It's a stretch, but it's good income and still manageable while maintaining a strong commitment to my family. According to these numbers, the reverse scale definitely works. Smaller truly is better. I haven't driven clients away. In fact, I've signed up scores of new clients. My little theory about small by design is panning out just fine.

However, my little theory doesn't matter if I gain income but the quality of my work goes down. We need to measure that element of success just as much as income. That is harder to quantify. At the beginning, the answer was a painfully obvious no. In my first six weeks on my own, I was fully blowing it. I was running way behind on projects, and clients were polite but clearly not impressed. When half of the e-mails in your inbox are asking you when a project will be completed, that's not good. I was spending as much time putting out fires for clients as I was doing actual legal work, and the freedom of time that I had was working against me. I'm not a naturally disciplined person. My mind was all over the place, and there was no boss riding me to keep me focused.

As of the end of my first full month on my own, my reverse scale wasn't working. Costs were down, and profits were up, but quality had fallen off a cliff. Then I hired a project manager, and everything turned around. My project manager is single-handedly responsible for my success as a solo attorney. It's funny how, at first, I was fully dedicated to operating entirely on my own. No associates. No paralegals. No staff. The source of this plan is so ridiculous that it's a little bit funny. In the movie *Sweet Home Alabama* with Reese Witherspoon, the main character is attempting to get her estranged husband to sign divorce papers, and eventually he does. She then proceeds to get married to her new fiancé (in Alabama, of course), and her little old solo attorney realizes that she never signed the papers herself and was about to get married even though she was never properly divorced. He panics, flies to Alabama, and runs to the ceremony, shouting to stop the proceedings. He arrives just in time, and I'll let you watch the movie to see the happy ending (spoiler alert).

That little old lawyer was my inspiration for running my little law practice completely by myself with no staff and no help from anyone. There was just one small problem: *it was a movie!* I may not be the world's top authority on running a small law practice, but I can tell you that you shouldn't base your future on a business plan you hatched from a Reese Witherspoon movie. I needed help. Based on my performance during my first month, my *Sweet Home Alabama* plan was a total disaster. I was genuinely afraid of losing my long-term clients.

Ten weeks into my new solo adventure, I hired my project manager. It took her a full month just to get my to-do list under control. After a while (when I let her do her job), we were operating as a fairly well-oiled machine. She moved on after about a year, and I now work with my wife every day. I still have my undisciplined moments. But whenever I would put my project manager or my wife into a position of authority over my tasks and calendar, I kept moving forward at the right pace and working on the right project. Overall, client satisfaction has dramatically improved. Delivering projects late is almost entirely a thing of the past. We are back to feeling like this was a good idea after all.

In my mind, the reverse scale is now working both on the income front as well as the quality front. I've gone from a twenty-five-attorney firm to a solo operation with my wife and daughter teaming up to help me run things. With that increase in quality, my referrals and repeat business have also increased. That is a more accurate sign that clients are happy. Most often, a client won't tell you when they are dissatisfied. They just won't call you again. My clients are calling again and again and referring more and more every month I'm on my own.

I'm finishing up the writing of this book in 2020, which is quickly becoming legendary for all the wrong reasons. The entire world is caught in the grip of a virus called coronavirus, and states and nations have effectively shut down the global economy. I'm repeatedly telling my kids, "No, girls, we've never seen anything like this before." There are runs on basic supplies in grocery stores. Small businesses which existed for decades are closing permanently. The stock market has collapsed. Schools are closed. High school and college graduations are cancelled, along with sporting events and concerts. I haven't eaten inside a restaurant in three months. I'm badly in need of a haircut. The world is vacillating between scary and infuriating, and it's taking a toll on professional service firms. I heard that one of the firms I used to work for cut attorney salaries by 20 percent across the board. Firms are laying off attorneys left and right. The most common term being used to describe 2020 so far is *dumpster fire*. I can't disagree.

The effect on me? Negligible. If anything, business is up a little. I just need to shut off the noise of a twenty-four-hour news cycle and social media and get the work done. I'm genuinely shocked. Business continues coming in. Clients are still paying their bills. I never had to hit the panic button. One of the myths of being a solo entrepreneur is that you are taking the maximum possible risk. In some ways, this is true. But there are a lot of ways that being a solo entrepreneur hedges significantly against risk, and the lack of repetitive monthly expenses is perhaps the most significant one of those hedges.

My monthly obligations are minimal. I honestly could have had my income cut in half without a major impact on my life because the biggest drain on my company's finances on a monthly basis is… me. When you scale a business, your revenue increases. That's what almost every entrepreneur wants. However, your costs also scale.

Your revenue can dry up quickly with a global pandemic afoot, but your costs don't disappear quite so quickly. Employees and landlords still want to be paid. Your bank still wants to you pay the interest on your operating line of credit. The government still wants their real estate taxes.

Even when the dumpster fire was at its maximum heat, I never went into panic mode because I simply don't have very many monthly obligations pulling at me. I can't imagine being at a firm with a monthly payroll obligation in the hundreds of thousands for all the non-equity attorneys and staff. And with everyone working from home, you're paying a staggering amount for rent on an empty office. I have none of that. I've never had to send, then, "Everyone is taking a pay cut" or "We're laying off half the staff" e-mail. I don't care how tough you are as an entrepreneur; telling someone their job is over because you can't afford to pay them is brutal.

I've sidestepped all of that because the expense of running a solo law firm out of your house is almost nothing. Here I am, sitting in my former living room, just like I have been since the day I went out on my own. I have no rent. My monthly ongoing obligations consist of a handful of subscription services, such as Microsoft and my online billing service. My malpractice insurance is a blistering $150 per month. Running a micro business results in running with micro risk. That sounds counterintuitive because, as noted, going out on your own is considered a total risk. However, there are a lot of attorneys with secure steady paychecks who just found out that their paycheck wasn't quite as secure as they thought.

I'm not convinced that traditional employment is less risky than entrepreneurship. In the middle of this pandemic, I see traditional employment as more of a risk than ever. I also see the traditional law firm structure being an exceptional risk with the mountain of monthly obligations that come along with it. I'm very happy in my reverse-scaled business model, and I've had to make surprisingly few adjustments. This pandemic has proven beyond a doubt that smaller really can be better.

If the concept of reverse scaling works even in an unprecedented reaction to a global pandemic, then how do you go about implementing it? Later in this book, I'll discuss the key elements of that transition, including building a book of business before you go out on your own, retaining those clients when you go solo, and setting up your operations in a way that is uniquely crafted to the way your mind works. And if you're anything like me, you'll jump forward to those chapters immediately, but let me try to slow you down a bit and get you to focus on starting with intentionality.

Freedom is perhaps one of the greatest aspects of going solo, but complete freedom to be whoever you want means you need to first figure out who you want to be, and that's not as simple as it sounds.

BLANK CANVAS

Redesigning Your Life Is Harder than You'd Think

We're so used to having to live within certain boundaries in traditional employment that we can struggle once the shackles have been cast off. Sure, you can do whatever you want, but where do we start? We can stare at that blank canvas for hours or weeks or years, and we never take the first step of designing our own new life from the ground up.

At a job, we know that there are certain benchmarks that we're supposed to hit in order to satisfy the boss. We also work within a specific job description. In some workplaces, if we stretch that job description, we're considered innovative. In others, we'd be considered annoying. But there aren't very many jobs, particularly in the professional service industries, where we're encouraged, or even permitted, to blow the doors off and truly innovate and be ourselves. Even the most progressive start-ups with pool tables and napping pods have a culture that you're expected to adapt into. It's rare in traditional employment that we're asked, or even permitted, to truly deviate from a well-defined path. We're not really allowed to design our work from a completely blank canvas.

But imagine that now you're out on your own. Freedom! Just you and a card table and a laptop, ready to conquer the world. At first, you see your new flexibility as the opportunity to wear cargo shorts or sweatpants to the office that used to be your living room, but that's not out of the box. That's barely nudging the edges of the box. At first, your sense of freedom is defined by the fact that you can do the same job you've been doing but in a slightly different way, at a different pace, different hours of the day, and in different clothes. Maybe even in your pajamas.[3]

After a while, you start seeing freedom as something bigger than just the means by which you complete your job. You start realizing that you can literally redefine everything about what you do. For me, I did what every solo does and started working in jeans and a T-shirt every day—this is particularly easy in an era where it's becoming somewhat rare to meet your clients face to face, at least in my type of legal practice. However, it didn't take long before I started to realize that I technically didn't need to practice law at all. I could invest in real estate. I could write books (the jury is still out on that one. Thoughts?), I could blog, invent some clever device, or pursue any number of other ways to earn a living; and no one is looking over my shoulder to be sure I'm not pursuing these other ventures while I'm on their clock. The prospect of developing other possible avenues of success in addition to your traditional practice becomes realistic.

Once you realize you have the ability to redefine what you do and not just how you do your previous job, you take it to the next level and realize you have the ability to entirely redefine who you are. This is where the true joy of going solo started to settle in for me. I really like spending time with my daughters, and at seventeen and twelve, they still like spending time with me. I was able to begin redefining myself as a dad. As opposed to the dad who had heartfelt explanations for missing events, I became the dad who attend those events. Instead of being the grinder who was bucking for partnership and getting in the office at 6:30 a.m., I was the dad who walked his daughter to the bus stop every day. I even cooked dinner every once in a while.

---

[3] Practicing law in your PJs can be fun, but remember to toss a button-down shirt on before that video conference at two o'clock, especially in 2020, the "Summer of Online Meetings." I've got some personal experience on that one that I'm still trying to banish from my memory.

It didn't stop there. I could be an athlete again because I don't need to get a permission slip from HR to go work out at noon every day. I could be a romantic again because I can slip out at lunch and buy my wife flowers from the shop down the street. I can become a reader. A wholistic health nut. I can smoke cigars at work (check with the spouse on that one). I can call clients or referral sources just to say hello, legitimately without any ulterior motive. I can refer business to people that I like instead of people on a prescribed list of referral partners prepared by a partnership subcommittee. I can charge clients what I want. I can write whatever I want in letters. I can do whatever I want with my website. I can post whatever I like on social media without coming into work the next day to an e-mail reminding me that my social media posts "are a reflection of the firm."

But in the midst of all this freedom, you find yourself staring at a blank canvas. You realize that you have don't actually have a lot of specifics regarding what you want to do, how you want to do it, and who you want to be; and you're suddenly driving down a superhighway with no guard rails. Forget guardrails, there aren't even lane markers. So you need to begin to figure it all out literally from scratch.

The freedom to be whatever you want is actually quite daunting and overwhelming once it becomes a reality. My advice is to embrace that blank canvas before jumping off the cliff of self-employment. This is one area where I could have done a better job of setting myself up for success before going solo. I just never expected to find that packing all that freedom into a manageable box would be so difficult.

One of the main temptations to going solo is to try to be a generalist. If you're going to be a lawyer, you want to handle small business, contracts, real estate, litigation, wills and trusts, and maybe even file the occasional trademark or two. Heck, you might even take a shot at defending the occasional DUI or traffic ticket. Your clients are about to be your sole source of income. You're losing your safety net, so the last thing you're going to do is turn down a client who needs your help. Whatever they need and in whatever practice area they need it, you'll be their guy.

That sounds so compelling. It sounds so right. Grab business wherever you can get it. But as we reviewed earlier, it's not the path to true freedom. The solo attorneys you see out there trying to handle all things for all people are almost all working their tails off just to survive. If you pursue a generalist business model, no matter what industry you're in, it won't take long before your solo practice feels more like a prison than your traditional nine-to-five job ever did.

The very first thing you need to do when (or before) going solo is to start to narrow down the scope of your expertise to those narrow areas where you can truly shine. Narrow your focus to the areas where you can deliver truly outstanding results to your clients. You will no longer be judged by a managing partner; you'll be judged by the value you deliver to your clients, and the only way to deliver genuine value is to provide a specific set of services based on your specific set of skills and gifts.

To start, look at everything you do in your job today, and start chopping out the various parts of your job that you'd like to avoid. We're not talking about laziness here. We're not just getting rid of a particular service area or practice group because it's hard; going solo is hard. What I'm talking about is chopping out those areas of your industry where you could work your fingers to the bone and still not stand out from the crowd. They don't allow you to shine. However, as a solo, you are your own beacon; there is no marketing department shining for you. You need to focus on areas of practice that let you shine because of your gifts and talents. Most often, this involves narrowing down your practice to areas you truly love and have a passion for.

Start thinking about how you can make a living at just those things. Being a jack of all trades and master of none doesn't excite anyone, least of all, you. Why not be excited about coming to work again? For me, and probably for most, it was easy to put together a list of the things I didn't like doing at my job. Let me walk you through my process of narrowing down my focus to see the process in action.

As a lawyer, I occasionally got a kick out of being involved on the outskirts of litigation, but I absolutely hate going to court.[4] Drafting lawsuits and motions was exciting, but there is not a huge market for attorneys who can draft a lawsuit but don't even know where to file it once it's done. Litigation is also ridiculously stressful. I respect litigation attorneys. The emotional roller coaster is not for me. So litigation was out.

"I hate litigation" isn't exactly a compelling business plan. I needed to keep cutting out practice areas. I hate legal research. A lot. And new grads are better at it anyway. That was easy. No legal research.

Litigation and research are out, so we're down to just transactional law. That's still a very broad description. Let's keep going narrower.

I don't know all the technical details of real estate transactions. I can handle the contracts, but I don't know much about title insurance, etc. At forty-seven years old, learning a brand-new area of the law is not my cup of tea. Real estate is out.

So now we're getting even more narrow. Litigation is a no. Transactional law is a yes but not real estate and not estate planning. We're getting even more focused now. I'm not just a transactional lawyer; I'm a corporate lawyer, and I hate huge companies, so I'm a corporate lawyer just for small business. When you separate the wheat from the chaff, what I'm left with is corporate law for small business. That's my sweet spot narrowly defined.

Fine. We've eliminated what I don't like and identified what's left over, but what do I like? Beyond just "whatever is left" after removing what I don't like, what are the things that I really enjoy doing? I love talking to clients on the phone. I really enjoy drafting a top-notch legal document, especially if a bit of creativity is required to get the

---

[4] When I interviewed for my last job, I explained to them that I didn't even know where all the courthouses are located. We laughed and laughed and had a good time. When the laughter died down, I paused for a moment and said, "I know how funny that sounds, but before you hire me, you should know that I wasn't kidding. I literally do not know where all the courthouses are." They hired me anyway.

job done right. I even like adding in little surprises like sticking the client's logo into the contract I'm drafting for them. I absolutely love working with clients who are being bullied and putting the bad guys in their place, and I like some of the nerdier portions of running an office like tracking the productivity numbers and building spread-sheets. I really nerd out on the spreadsheets.

I looked at all of this introspection and started to build what my practice would look like. Then I started implementing that while I was still working a traditional job. I started reducing my practice to the areas that I knew I could handle on my own and weaning myself off the need for those tasks that didn't really appeal to me, remembering that once I'm on my own, there is no one down the hall to ask questions if I get in over my head. So toward the end of my employment, I essentially reformulated my entire practice into something I could manage on my own into areas where I wouldn't have a lot of questions or a significant need to seek out help from others. During this time, maintaining the steady paycheck allowed me to take some risks here and there along the way before diving headfirst into the deep end of the entrepreneurial pool.

With my job essentially redefined and having worked out the details of actually pulling it off on my own, I stepped out of the warm relaxing waters of unemployment and quit my job. After a few months, I started recognizing the next phase of my transformation into a true entrepreneur. I could not only redefine what I do and how I do it but also who I am, and I began again by looking at the negative. I didn't like that I'd gotten to be a hundred pounds overweight. I didn't like that I was wasting hours upon hours every day, mindlessly staring into a cell phone. I didn't like that I had stopped going to church and teaching kids classes there. I didn't like how much fast food I was eating. I didn't like that I was tired…all the time.

It's probably fair to say that I'm still sorting my way through this second phase. I'm taking more time to eat what I need instead of what I want, and the pounds are drifting off slowly. I'm exercising because I enjoy it as opposed to cramming myself into the car and forcing myself to go to the gym because I'm supposed to. I'm reading almost every day, and I'm going to church almost every Sunday. We actually started having friends over to the house again. It had been literally years since anyone other than family had been over just to hang out. I started focusing on having fun. I can honestly admit that I had genuinely forgotten how to do that. How pathetic is that? But honestly, that's a reality for a lot of people trying to squeeze a life in around the edges of a traditional job that demands a high number of billable hours every year.

My encouragement to you in this chapter is to start looking at all of that before you walk out on your steady paycheck. I take credit for thinking ahead enough to start redefining my practice into something I could manage on my own before quitting my job, but I think I'd be months ahead of the game if I had put a bit more thought into the "who do I want to be" questions as opposed to looking at those for the first time a few months into going solo.

Grab a sheet of paper, and just start jotting things down. Talk to your spouse. Talk to your kids. Give them all a true vote and really listen to what they have to say. Start mapping out what it will look like to be on your own as the person you really want to be. But be patient; it doesn't come all at once. I still, to this day, talk to my wife and ask what she thinks we should be doing for fun this summer, and she's honest and says she has no idea because the ability to plan whatever we want is so new to us. We're still navigating it. So navigate earlier than I did.

It's funny. Like everything else in my life, writing this book is taking longer than I thought it would; and over the course of that time, my thoughts on what it means to be free and what I want my life to look like have changed. Remember that the vision of what your life will be is a living thing; it shouldn't be rigid. You should spend some time really thinking through what your vision is for freedom *at the beginning of your practice*. However, understand that the vision will change over time.

You need to find a balance between refusing to change a vision that needs updating versus walking away from a vision just because you've hit a roadblock. It is easy to vacillate between these two extremes. On the one side, you are so open-minded about changing your vision that it hardly counts as a vision at all. The first time you face a challenge as an entrepreneur is solved by changing your vision. Clients aren't coming in as quickly as you thought they would in your specific field, so you abandon that field and shift toward being more of a generalist. Be careful about that. Don't be so overly flexible in defining your vision that you walk away from it every time a challenge or distraction steps in front of you.

The other extreme is the entrepreneur who is so bent on his vision that he's entirely incapable of seeing that it's just not working but refusing to change or update the vision to something that works or something that the marketplace truly needs. For me, my initial vision was that I would always be operating 100 percent on my own without any staff. I was very dedicated to this vision. I romanticized the solitude of this business model, and I worked at it pretty hard. I was being stubborn and was not willing to see the possibility that change was needed. I was falling into the too rigid category, and I made the classic error of my vision being too detailed.

Visions are large things, guiding concepts, and values-based maps to lead us to a large end goal. But my vision wasn't large concepts; it was details of the actual process, and this is a mistake. If your vision includes such finite details as "working on a laptop in my living room," that's too narrow; and since you've filed it away in your mind as your vision, then you'll probably be stubborn about changing it.

When I stepped back and really looked at what my vision was, I was able to cast aside the details and focus on the larger values I was pursuing. In reality, my vision wasn't to work by myself in cargo shorts and a T-shirt in my living room; those things, and other details, were the by-products or results of my vision. My true vision, stripped of the details I tacked on, was to do good work for clients, choose to work with clients I liked, spend more time with my family, and provide for them well. That is a vision I can be stubborn about.

However, the details and mechanisms of how to get there need to be flexible. As you set out to decide what your life is going to look like once you begin living it from the perspective of a blank canvas, do your best to separate the true core concepts of what is important to you; and set them apart from the details of how you'll get there because if there is anything I've learned from going solo, it's that the details of how you get there are almost always going to surprise you. But no matter how much those details change, you want to be sure that you're always moving in the direction of those core values that drove you to walk away from traditional employment in the first place.

Once you've taken some time to build your vision for your business, it's time to start thinking about how you're going to pay the bills. Your vision includes the type of clients you want to work with, but you need a plan for how to attract that type of client. In short, you're going to need to do the one thing that most people avoid like the plague: you're going to need to sell—and you can.

DON'T FREAK OUT BUT... YOU'RE GOING TO NEED TO SELL

For most people in the professional services industries (and every other industry for that matter), the thought of selling is so negative that we can't even call it selling. We call it *business development* or marketing, networking, or just about anything other than *sales*. Some are good at it, but we don't call them top salesman. We call them cool names like *rainmakers*. We absolutely, positively, avoid the word *sales*. So let's get right down to it.

If you are going to succeed as a solo, you're going to need to sell. We're not going to be afraid of that word in this chapter, and we're not going to call you a rainmaker. We're not going to call it business development; we're going to call it sales because that's what it is, and we're going to call you a salesman because that's who you are. More importantly, we're going to debunk all of the garbage in your head that makes you hate the thought of being called a salesperson, because sales is great. It's a rush, and you can do it. You can actually be great at it without transforming your personality. In fact, being who you genuinely are in your heart is the number one key to being great at sales, which is why the last chapter is where it is in this book. So let's sell some professional services and have fun doing it.

What Selling Isn't: No Arm-Twisting Allowed

Before you panic and slam the book shut, let's go over a few common misconceptions that make people hate the concept of selling:

- Selling is *not* the process of getting people to buy something they don't want.
- Selling does not require you to change your personality into a nonstop extrovert.
- Sales allows you (*requires* you) to be yourself.

The thing that scares everyone about selling, especially in the professional services field, is that no one wants to take on the persona of the used car salesman within a professional context. As professionals, we're supposed to be different. We're supposed to be professional, and that doesn't leave any room for closing questions like, "What is it going to take to get you to sign my retainer agreement right now?" Holy Lord, please don't ever say that to a potential client.

If that phrase and the thought of actually saying it to a prospective client makes you want to puke, that's good because that's not real sales. That's a slick line intended to take advantage of the vulnerable and the weak. As professionals, our job is to advocate for our clients, not to trick them into doing something they don't want to do. We advocate for our clients. We protect them. We fight for them. We get pissed off at the things that piss them off. They trust us with the most important aspects of their lives. We're on the same side as our clients, so we do not ever (ever) begin a relationship by twisting anyone's arm.

Let's stop for a reality check. Don't take the soft sales approach too far. There will be times that you are meeting a potential client for the first time, and you genuinely believe that they need to move quickly to resolve whatever issue they have presented to you. Perhaps you're an attorney meeting with someone bumping up against the statute of limitations on a claim or CPA meeting someone who just had their accounts seized by the IRS or a business coach meeting with someone who is about to lose three key team members. You know they have to retain an attorney quickly, but from a pure sales perspective, they don't have to hire *you*. In this case, there is nothing wrong with twisting their arm to take action now. Right now. That's actually your job. You don't want to be so laid back in your sales approach that you fail to convey the urgency of their situation, but you also need to accept that the urgency is to hire *someone*. There is no urgency that they hire *you*; convey the urgency to act. However, when it comes to deciding whether you're the right lawyer, accountant, or coach to take them through that process, that's sales; and we don't ever twist arms when it comes to sales.

If we're not working to get someone to buy something they don't want, what *are* we doing? It's very simple, and very misunderstood: we're *connecting*. That's it. We're making connections. Let's start with an analogy.

You're an American, and you're in Paris for a business meeting or vacation or whatever. You've overcome jet lag, and you're out of the shower. Time to get pretty (or handsome if you're more into that) for whatever your day has in store for you. So you grab your hair dryer, and as anyone who has travelled to Europe can tell you, the plug doesn't fit. It's a pretty simple problem really. Hair dryers in Paris do exactly the same thing as hair dryers in Cleveland, Ohio, but the plugs are different. So now you have an option. The stereotype of sales would dictate that you do everything in your power to convince the Paris-style outlet to accept your Cleveland-style plug. You'll be persuasive, "C'mon, receptacle. It's all just electricity. Why not accept my plug?" Then you'll build a sense of urgency. "I have a meeting in forty-five minutes, and I can't go in there with wet hair. You have three minutes to accept my Cleveland-style plug." You may even try the other smarmy sales tricks we all hate, like tossing in a bit of guilt and shame. "Do you know how many weeks it's taken me to get this meeting arranged, and now you're pulling this on me?"

Does this analogy seem entirely ridiculous? Of course. The two plugs simply aren't a fit. The key is to bring a plug and an outlet together that are already a fit for one another. We don't attempt to reshape either to begrudgingly fit into the other. If you think there is no point in trying to "twist the arm of a plug to get it to fit into an outlet," you'd be right. What you need to understand is that it's no more effective with human beings. This process of finding the right fit is *real sales*. Making a connection. And anyone can do that, even people who are terrified of what they *think* sales is about.

Sales is 100 percent purely, and nothing more than, the process of identifying what it is that you offer and the unique way in which you offer it and connecting yourself to people who need that and fit well with that unique way of doing things. That's it. If you are doing sales correctly, you never need to persuade a potential client to hire you. Your job is to be sure that they know what you can do and who you are and *find out* if that is a match for what they need. Notice I emphasized the term *find out*. Your mission is not to convince people you're the right solution for them; your mission is to connect with people, and when it's a fit, you've made a sale.

There is no need to change who you are to ensure you are the right for a prospective client. Just like the plug, the key is to find a receptacle that is already a correct fit. Adapting your personality or trying to become someone you are not rarely works at all, and when it does, it's always temporary. Prospective clients can smell a fake personality a mile away. Service industries rely on your ability to quickly establish trust with a prospective client. Displaying a facade is the opposite of establishing trust.

Banish the image of the stereotypical used car salesman from your mind, and understand that the "coffee is for closers" speech from *Glengarry Glen Ross* is for entertainment purposes only. Side note: if you haven't seen that scene, head over to YouTube, and check it out. It's quite fantastic. It's very, very wrong, but it's awesome in its own way.

What we're going to touch on in this chapter is real sales for high-end service businesses like CPAs, attorneys, coaches, consultants, etc. We'll do the best we can in a single chapter, and it will be enough to get you going. However, the topic of genuinely ethical and effective high-end sales is at least a book, if not a series of books, but we'll at least get a start here.

What Sales Is: Finding Connections

Selling is the simple process of connecting what you have to the people who need it. If you've ever seen a photo of a huge computer data room, there are colored cables going in every direction. Thousands of them. Every cable has a simple job: connect one thing to another thing. To the layman who has never worked with cables, it looks like a tangled mess and is instantly overwhelming. If you asked the average person to walk into that data room and check the wire that connects the thingy to the whatsit, we would have no clue where to start. But then, the technician goes in. He sees the room entirely differently. He is calm and relaxed because he understands the environment where he is standing. He is not overwhelmed and knows exactly what to do. He knows where the thingy is, where the whatsit is, and how to find the cable that connects them. He knows how to check to be sure the cable is working and can even tell you if the type of cable being used is the right one for the job. Sales is exactly the same way. In sales, you are the thingy. We're trying to connect you to the client, which is the whatsit. And the cable? That's your sales pitch.

Compatibility

Most people who don't understand sales entirely skip the first step. We first need to be sure that the thingy we have (you) is compatible with the whatsit we're talking to (the client). The stress of sales comes from one very simple error: you're trying to connect yourself with someone that just doesn't fit. In our data room example, our technician can tell you that you can't connect two incompatible machines no matter what kind of cable you use; it just won't work. But in sales, we dig our heels in and become obsessed with the goal of closing a sale with whoever is standing in front of us. We keep switching out cables (our sales pitch), determined to find the cable that can connect these two incompatible devices. If we could just find the right sales pitch, then clients would hire us. However, that's not how it works. The connection should be simple. The cable, your sales pitch, should fit comfortably into both devices. When we make a genuine connection with someone, we often say, "We just clicked right away," just like the cable that clicks right into the thingy (you) and just as easily clicks into the whatsit (your client). You didn't have to force it. You didn't have to buy an adapter. It just fit. It wasn't a matter of forcing the cable to work. It was a matter of finding two devices that were compatible with one another. That's sales. Identification, not persuasion.

If you're finding that you need to twist arms to close clients, then you're going about it all the wrong way. You just need to head out into the marketplace and find the clients who are the perfect fit for you. Without you changing and without them changing, you just…click. This is true in any sales environment, but it is particularly true in the service industries.

I was confronted with this compatibility issue early on in my career. My personality is very informal. I like to crack jokes. I mainly like to crack jokes about myself, and I'm never hesitant to crack a joke about lawyers in general. I unofficially brand myself as the lawyer who doesn't like lawyers. "We make things more complicated than they need to be," I quip, and it gets a good laugh, eases the tension in the room, and I can start having a more genuine connection with the potential client I'm meeting with. *Usually…*

I was in a meeting with Jay and doing what I normally do. I was lighthearted and cracking the occasional cute joke, and I thought I was knocking it out of the park with this potential client. He looked like he had just stepped off a surfboard. Dreadlocks. Tan. Hawaiian shirt, shorts, and flip flops. Any guy who shows up to a meeting with a lawyer looking like this guy is going to like the fun lawyer Jim Voigt in a second. I knew I had this guy. Except I didn't.

Jay was a very informal guy, but he wasn't looking for an informal lawyer. He took my casual approach to the conversation as an indication that I didn't really know what I was doing, that I was chatting my way through a meeting and avoiding the harder details of his case because I couldn't handle them. The fact is that Jay's case was right in the middle of my sweet spot, and I could have done a great job for him, but the failure of the two of us to connect prevented him from every seeing that.

The thingy (me) was very much not compatible with the whatsit (Jay). Jay actually left the meeting angry. Talk about blowing it on an initial client consult. I was so focused on "just me being me, bro" that I never really stopped to listen to what Jay had to say. I also looked at his appearance and made a lot of wild assumptions about what type of person he was. All rookie mistakes. Yes, Jay had a transactional matter that was in my sweet spot, but Jay was not relaxed about it at all. He had a problem with his real estate investment. A problem with the title or the method in which he took ownership of it, and he was stressed about it. This was not a calm, cool, "no problemo, bro" surfer in front of me. This was a guy who was scared that he had made a permanent mistake with his real estate that couldn't be fixed. In reality, this problem was actually pretty easy to fix, but in my rush to be the coolest dude in the room, I totally missed the fact that Jay didn't see this as a quick fix and just needed a lawyer to handle it. Jay was scared and needed reassurance that the lawyer he was talking to could actually deliver the solution he needed. I didn't deliver that confidence.

What's my point? My point is that I was not genuinely myself in this meeting. It was early on in my career, perhaps my third year out of law school, and I was overplaying my self-declared amazing ability to connect with clients. I didn't stop to listen. I honestly didn't even take the time to read Jay's body language and look into his eyes. I didn't pause to genuinely care about what Jay was going through, and honestly, this wasn't my true personality. I had constructed this vision I had of myself as a laidback lawyer that the average guy would really connect to, and I brought that fabrication into the conference room instead of just being Jim Voigt. I tried to force the connection with Jay instead of just listening to what he had to say, being myself in my response, and describing the solution to his problem. I was a slick salesman, not a lawyer ready to serve someone who needed his help.

What I was doing with Jay was called *mirroring*. It is a sales technique whereby you make yourself look and act like the person you are selling to. If that sounds like a load of garbage, it is. It works very well when selling bicycles or low-cost term life insurance. It does not have any place in the sales process for professional services in my opinion. Some may disagree with me on that one, and that's okay.

The key is honesty. Just be yourself. That sounds like the type of advice that a mom would give her junior high nerd son on the first day of school (not that I have any *personal* experience with that), and it's true here for all the same reasons. However, there is a far more practical aspect to the need for honesty in service industry sales; you're going to have plenty to keep track of running your new business. The last thing you need to do is try to keep track of which of your many personalities you dished out to a client the last time you spoke with them.

Up to now, we've only been discussing one aspect of sales, closing the deal. You have a client sitting in front of you or on the phone, and you need to put your best foot forward to let them know that you're the right fit for their need, but we've completely glossed over the question of how to get that potential client sitting across from you in the first place.

How do you meet potential clients? There are a lot of books out there on this topic, and in all honesty, the answer really depends on what type of business you are. In the law, the douchebags of our industry look down on personal injury lawyers (until they get T-boned at a busy intersection) because they put up huge billboards that read "Injured at work?" and they always have a 1-800 number to call. This type of advertising is considered *beneath* the lofty erudite windbags billing huge corporations at $800 an hour, but guess what, those billboards and the cheesy TV ads these guys run actually work. It's why they use them. So the main takeaway for this section is to encourage you to try different ways to bring people in and get them on the phone. I'll be describing what has worked for me, and I think you should try it. I really do think it's the best way, but I'm not done experimenting myself, so I'm not going to claim my way is the best way for everyone.

I've tried a lot of different techniques to get butts in seats. I've given continuing legal education seminars to other attorneys, taught classes at the local community college, sent out thousands of direct mail pieces, and I actually got on WGN radio one time, one of the biggest listening audiences in the world. Before I was in the law, I did cold-calling. I've built social media followings. I've blogged. I've done a lot of networking. Through all of that, I have found one consistent thread that has brought be the most success, and my suspicion is that it's true for anyone in the service industries. I don't recruit clients; I recruit referral sources. That's so critically important. I'm going to repeat it: I don't recruit clients; I recruit referral sources.

I can earn thousands of dollars in fees from a single client, so it would make sense for me spend a lot of time recruiting for clients because getting one client really pays off. However, that flushes out the paradox of the service industries. In general, we sell our time. We bill by the hour. So all of those hours trying to find and connect with a single client are far more expensive than they feel. It's a massive waste of time that doesn't pay off even if you're good at it.

I've been doing this for fifteen years now, and I support my family, a paralegal and a very well-paid project manager with my book of business. I've got a good book of business. And you know what I've never done once in those fifteen years? I've never once taken a potential client to lunch. Not once. But don't get me wrong; I've done plenty of lunches, but those lunches have all been with potential *referral sources*, not potential *clients*. I've even done plenty of lunches with existing clients to thank them for their business. Why? Because every client you have is a referral source. They're your best referral source, actually.

Listen, I'll try stuff. I'll do a direct mail campaign. In fact, I'm drafting a new letter for a direct mail campaign this weekend. However, that's minimal effort. I write the letter, and my staff runs with it from there. The meetings, the lunches, the coffees, they are all so time-consuming that you need to be sure you're getting value out of that time you spend.

Meeting with a referral source can mean literally dozens of clients over the years. I have one referral source who sends me new clients almost every week. Was the time I spent with him at a Starbucks worth my time? Oh, heck yeah. I'm thinking of changing my daughter's name to Don in his honor.

There is second aspect to recruiting referral sources that makes a lot more sense than recruiting clients directly. Recruiting clients means you know absolutely nothing about the person you are finally meeting with. It's an absolute toss of the dice as to whether you're going to be a good fit with one another. You're hoping like crazy that your Clevelandian plug isn't going to have found a target that's Parisian. But in the end, if you're trying to build your business by finding clients, you have no idea. You're gambling.

Recruiting referral sources is so radically different. Why? Because the referral source knows you, and in most cases, at least in some ways, you're probably similar in personality. I've seen people dispute this, but in my experience, people tend to hire people who are like themselves. Also, referral sources tend to refer clients to people who are like themselves.

My top referral source and I are very similar in personality, and the clients he sends me are also of a very similar personality. We didn't sit down and strategize this; it's just human nature. People refer clients to people who they like and who are like themselves. It's as simple as that. So the clients that you get from a referral source are going to be dramatically more likely to hire you once they meet you because, to a certain extent, they've been vetted by your referral source to be a good match. Your closing ratio (the number of clients you meet vs. the number of clients who hire you) will go through the roof all because of plain old human nature.

In my experience, the best way to meet referral sources is through networking groups. Perhaps you hate networking groups. It might be the type of group you're in. I hate networking groups that require you to bring in a certain number of referrals to each meeting. That is a recipe for one simple scenario: some guy sitting in his car in the parking lot outside the chamber of commerce office, desperately scrolling through his phone to find some idiot he can refer to someone so he doesn't have to put a dollar in the no referral jar. No, thanks! I don't want that referral.

It's important to consider the time commitment involved in networking correctly. Networking groups take time. People refer clients to people they like and people they trust (more on this below), but the point right now is that it takes time to build relationships with the members of your networking group so that they will like you and trust you.

My most successful networking group I ever attended didn't refer a single client to me for the first six months, and while I maintain that networking is the right way to build your practice, I say that with the understanding that it's very time-consuming. So you need to match the group you join with the time commitment that's appropriate for where you are in your career.

Early on, a weekly networking group might make sense for a few reasons: First, you need practice. Getting in front of a group of people and developing your elevator pitch is great practice, and a weekly networking group gives you a lot of practice. Second, until your book of business may not be at full capacity and you have the time. Also, meeting every week means you can form some tight bonds with the people in the group.

At the current stage in my career (about fifteen years in), my book of business doesn't really allow for weekly networking meetings. I've tried, actually. I just recently had to eat crow and retract my commitment to join a weekly group. My assumption was that it would be fine because it meets at 7:30 a.m. and wouldn't really interfere with my day, but two weeks in a row, my workload has made it impossible to attend (or, to be honest, not a great idea to attend). So I've decided to stick to my gut and avoid weekly networking meetings.

The key is to experiment. I reached that conclusion based on actual experience combined with a gut feel, but not just based on my assumptions or gut feel about it.

Once you've identified one or more networking groups that you like, your final decision in choosing a group has to do with the people in the group. How lively is the group? I've walked into a few networking group meetings and wondered who sucked the life out of the room before I got there. These were not people who were excited about being in business. The attendees should be high-energy, reaching out to you to welcome you as the new guy (or new gal) in the room. Look for lots of eye contact. If the entire room seems like it could use a group level antidepressant, then you should probably look elsewhere.

The next thing to look out for is people playing at being in business for themselves. These are people working full-time or part-time jobs, but they are at the group representing a side business that they run. These are most likely good people, but they haven't taken the full plunge and dedicated themselves to supporting their family with their business. It's certainly possible that folks like this can make strong referrals. It can happen. But in my experience, they typically do not; and worse, they generally will hit you up and ping your e-mail or even text you for referrals on a constant basis.

Finally, look at the character of those in the group. You're looking for *givers*. These are people who go into the group each week, doing everything they can to deliver value to people in that group. They are more interested in delivery referrals *to other members* as opposed to ensuring they get referrals *from the group*. And yes, you had better be a giver as well. Ironically, putting together a group of selfless networking partners can be the most beneficial for your business. It's the "Zig" Ziglar approach: to get what you want, help as many other people as possible get what they want. Walking into a networking group obsessed with the desire to bring value to the other members is key, and be sure to surround yourself with people of the same mindset.

There is some debate about this, but as noted earlier, my experience has been that people refer clients to people who they like and trust. Notice that I didn't say people refer clients to people who are very good at what they do. The purpose of a networking group is to establish relationships with the other people in the group. It is not simply a forum for you to convince strangers that you are an expert in your field by delivering a mind-blowing show of technical mastery.

A simple fact of life is that you are probably far more interested in your own field than the average person. So your technical wow factor is probably far more exciting to you than to the people you're talking to. Yes, you do want people in a networking group to know get a general idea that you know what you're doing, but I've made an interesting observation over my years in networking: people will refer clients to you on the assumption that you know what you're doing even if you've never proven it to them. The basic assumption is that you are an expert in your field. The test at a networking group is whether you are likeable and trustable.

The desire to display technical proficiency is natural. You probably judge yourself based on the quality of the services you provide to your clients. Your deliverables need to be technically correct; it's what makes you good at your job. Your clients will be relying on you to get them right, but the trick is that your clients won't actually know if the deliverables you provide are correct or not. You're the expert, not them. So the pressure is on for you to deliver top-notch stuff because there is no backstop. There is nothing other than your own knowledge preventing you from delivering something that's wrong or doesn't work or fails to cover all possible outcomes, etc. So technical proficiency is important! And you're good at the technical stuff, so let's get into that networking meeting and talk about the skill with which you delivered that last software solution. Let's get into the weeds and describe some of the more subtly artistic solutions you put into place that the average software engineer either wouldn't do or couldn't do. Let's convey to this room of potential clients that you are the master of your trade. Or...let's not.

You will score a few points. You'll come across as an expert, and that's important. You may even look like you're excited about your profession, and that's also important, but you'll have missed the opportunity to connect with people on a personal level. That, in the end, is the number one key to effective networking. You need to connect with people.

I met a guy, M, at a networking meeting. M was a seriously smart guy. I would suspect that he's almost certainly a genius (whatever the technical definition of that might be). M provides some kind of service that helps super rich people avoid paying a lot of taxes, and it appears to involve the use of complex life insurance products and strategies. I have absolutely no idea how those strategies work despite the fact that M went into great detail about every aspect of his services during his four-minute elevator pitch at a networking meeting I used to co-facilitate. Keep in mind that I'm a lawyer who deals with tax all the time, and I used to sell life insurance in a former life. So if there was anyone in that room who had a decent shot at understanding what M was talking about, it was me, and I was lost.

I walked away from that meeting knowing one very simple fact: there was no way I was ever going to put this guy on the phone with one of my clients. He seemed nice enough, but he obviously had no idea how to have real conversations with people. I was pretty intrigued in his solutions though. So I followed up with him to try to better understand his services. I even tried to serve up a referral on a silver platter and asked him to just shoot me an e-mail with a four-year-old level explanation of what he does and he couldn't. He just could not separate himself from the highly technical aspects of what he did for a living.

In contrast, we have C. C is probably also a genius. He's an actuary, and to this day, I don't fully get what an actuary does. It's exceptionally technical and involves complex tax stuff, and C knows it inside and out. He's really good at his job, and I know this. If you are a small business owner with a least a couple of employees, C can help you save more into a retirement plan than you could on your own through an IRA or even a 401(k). Those cap you out at about $50,000 a year in savings. C can put a plan in place that lets you save five times that much. How? I have no idea. However, I know it works and I have referred clients to C. I've also had lunch with C. Why? Because C is a genuinely nice guy, and I like him. If you've been paying attention, people refer clients to people they like. Get it?

C and M are probably equally good at their respective jobs, but I was never able to connect with M because his head was so wrapped up in the technical aspects of his job. C, on the other hand, was just a nice, personable guy who really let people get to know his true personality and connect. He delivered *just enough* technical know-how during meetings that we knew there was a ton of value buried under that nice guy persona.

This leads to my final point on sales and is especially important at networking meetings and chamber of commerce functions, etc. You need to be sure that people know what you do, and you need to be able to deliver that information in a single simple sentence. I've actually struggled with this. I got a call from a client one time who always had me prepare his corporate minutes and annual report each year. He was thinking of ditching his big downtown law firm because they had quoted him $94,000 in legal fees to help him buy a business. He asked me if I ever handled the sale or purchase of a business. Yes! It's one of the biggest parts of my legal practice. How could he not know this? Simple. I never told him.

It reminds me of something that people always struggle with at networking meetings. It is surprisingly difficult to get people at networking meetings to tell you who they can help. The most common answer is, "I can help anyone." This is also the most useless answer. I understand the temptation. When you are specific about who you can help, you feel like you're cutting off the possibility of working with people who are just slightly outside that scope of services, but this is wrong thinking. You need to be specific about who you can help. People will never refer business to someone on the basis that they can help anyone because inherently, we know that simply isn't true. I could easily say that I can help any small business owner with his legal needs, but that's not true. It's almost true. I can do a lot, but in reality, I don't do patent work. I don't handle litigation. I could probably handle a commercial real estate project, but there are people out there much better than me. So if I stick to my guns and say I can help anyone, I'm going to get referrals for areas that I don't handle and thoroughly underwhelm the client, and then…no more referrals from that referral source.

I used to run a networking group with a great insurance guy named Stephen, and he would press people to answer this simple question: "What will we hear people saying they would tell us to refer them to you?" It's a great question, and almost nobody could answer it. You'd hear answers like, "I can help people with their computer problems," but that's not answering the question that Stephen asked, is it? Or they would answer, "You'll hear them say they need a new computer network tech." Okay, we're getting closer, but that only covers those situations where people reach out and directly ask you to refer them a particular type of vendor. Better…but still not there.

That elusive question: "What will we hear people say that will tell us we need to refer them to you?" We would really struggle with this question at the networking group, but Stephen was relentless about it because he knew that it was a powerful question *when answered correctly.* Finally, at one meeting, there was a breakthrough. We had a handyman/carpenter in the group named Brian. In answering Stephen's question, Brian said, "You might hear them complain about a door that sticks or lets in cold air." Eureka! We have a winner. This seems so simple, but it's actually very hard to pull off. As correct as this answer was, it was also risky. The normal thought for an entrepreneur is to worry. "Now they are all going to think that all I do is fix doors. I'll lose all the referrals for kitchen remodels, decks, and additions." However, you need to understand that you're just wrong about that.

In sales, you are not looking to inform people about every possible service you might be able to offer; people simply can't remember that much data. If you overwhelm them with information, then they just won't bother referring clients to you. Your goal, instead, is to create a memory hook. Something that sticks in their mind and will pop to the front of their memory when triggered by something they've heard.

What about Brian? He finally answered the questions correctly, so did he get referrals? He did! They started flooding in, actually. People started asking *closing questions* or questions that lead directly to buying. People asked him follow up questions like, "Do you do anything else like kitchens or decks?" Yes! Ironically, if he had rattled off ten different things he can do (including kitchens and decks), then he would never have created the memory hook needed to prompt someone to refer to him when they have a chance to do so; but by creating that one memory hook, something that all of us have heard someone say or even experience ourselves, and answering a few follow-up questions, people had cemented into their mind exactly what Brian did for a living, and the referrals poured in after that.

For me, my practice is split into two parts: I held small businesses with most of what they need in terms of legal services, and I help people develop and structure real estate investments in senior housing, particularly by doing so with *OPM* or *other people's money*. I could describe myself as someone who helps people incorporate a new business, negotiate leases, shareholder agreements, form LLCs, loan documents, demand letters, operating agreements, licensing, trademark, wills, trusts, asset protection, and contracts.

Here's a test. Close your eyes, and (without cheating) name five things on that list that I just gave you, and you literally just read the list two seconds ago. Loading you up with a laundry list of what I do is not helpful, and it doesn't give you the information you need to refer clients to me. So instead, I say something very simple that sticks in the mind: "I help small businesses launch, grow, and exit. I help people develop assisted living projects with OPM." What happens next? Without fail, the very next comment will be, "What's OPM?" Then we're off to the races. Now they are asking questions, and we're engaged in conversation as opposed to me just rattling off an endless list of services that they'll never remember, and a month later, it's even better. "Hey, Jim, what did OPM stand for?" The memory hook is secure. I'm stuck in their mind even if they don't remember 100 percent of what I told them.

This is so counterintuitive for new business owners or people who have just gone solo. You're terrified of the thought of missing a business opportunity, but you're wrong. It's that simple. People will pay for a specialist. They don't like paying for someone who is a jack of all trades. Be specific about what you do; let people know what you do, and do so in a simple way that is stripped to the bone and easy to remember.

One key to doing so is to focus on the problem you solve as opposed to the service you provide. This will always be more memorable and help to generate better referrals. Brian could have said, "People will say they want a new door." Wrong! No one says that. Instead, he focused on the problem he solves. "People will say that their door sticks or lets in cold air." Being blunt, very few people care about how you will solve their problem; they just want to know you can solve it.

In my business, I can say, "I draft shareholder agreements that create multiple classes of voting and nonvoting shares and controlling the appointment of board members and officers and establish specific corporate actions that require shareholder consent." Wow. That really rolls off the tongue, doesn't it? Then how about this? "If you need investors, I can keep you in control of your company even if you have to give away more than half the shares." It's a dramatic improvement over a list of services I could provide because it speaks directly to what the client wants. You don't need to communicate the tasks you will perform; you need to communicate the fact that you understand what their true needs are, and that you have the ability to meet those needs in a way that they can trust.

COUNTING LIVES
CHANGED, NOT MONEY

Now that we've established your ability to sell effectively when you're on your own, we need to set the framework around what drives you to succeed as a solo professional. Despite what you would assume after reading the last chapter on sales, it's not money (spoiler alert). There will come a time that the money doesn't really mean that much to you anymore. Then what? This chapter answers that question.

So far in this book, I haven't really let my true feelings show through about being bumped off the partnership track at my first firm (twice). I was angry and bitter. It was part of what fueled my ignorant move to give same-day notice of my resignation. I walked into work every day feeling like I was never going to be enough for them, and I became bitter about the fact that I was billing as much or more than my peers and bringing in substantially more business.

I started to feel vindicated when I went out on my own because I was putting up productivity numbers that were more than enough for me to live on. I had given myself a pretty substantial raise by going solo, and I was starting to feel good about myself. That's rare for me. That feeling of vindication shone through when I said what I thought was a fairly benign statement to a friend of mine who had also gone solo.

Don is a shockingly successful residential real estate attorney in downtown Chicago. Residential real estate is a tough way to earn a living, but Don has genuinely mastered it. He was more than thrilled when I announced that I was going solo. "It's about time!" He has been one of my biggest supporters and loudest cheerleaders. Don is amazing, and wise.

I was talking to Don about finally feeling like I'm not a loser on a daily basis, and I said, "Yeah, I guess my $30K a month revenue wasn't good enough for them, but it's good enough for me." Vindication isn't any fun unless you can share your bitterness with a close friend, right? I was expecting Don to chime in and take a dig at my former firm as well. He didn't. He said, "Hey, I've been doing this on my own for a while now, and there is nothing better. The money is good; that's definitely true, but let me coach you up a little bit on something that's important. Is that okay?" This is what Don always says in response to me saying something dumb.

I was ready for it and said, "Yeah, sure." I had no idea what to expect.

"Listen, don't ever measure your success by revenue earned. Measure it by lives changed."

That hit me like a ton of bricks. In an instant, I felt petty; and let's be honest, I was being petty. So feeling petty was exactly where I needed to be. When you go solo, people will give you advice non-stop (some people even write an entire book full of it). Some of that advice will be burned into your memory, and this line from Don was one of those lines that I'll remember forever: "Don't measure your success by revenue earned. Measure it by lives changed."

That line is literally the reason that I'm writing this book. I'm absolutely obsessed with the freedom that I've achieved by going solo, and I want to change the lives of others who are crying out for that same freedom. It's why I launched a solo attorney incubator and started plucking people one at a time out of the doldrums of law firm existence into the free lifestyle I currently enjoy.

If you measure your success strictly by revenue earned, it's not going to take long before you feel like working for yourself is even worse than working for the worst boss you ever had. At least, when you had a regular job, you could go home at night and disconnect. Having the freedom to design your life to be whatever you want it to be should be filled with a passion for bringing value into people's lives. If it's nothing more than a push for cash, then you'll find yourself thinking about rejoining the workforce before you know it. How do I know that? Because I've wandered in and out of pursuing cash ever since going solo. It's only natural. Going solo doesn't suddenly launch you into a fantasy world where you don't have to worry about paying the bills. Going solo is pretty expensive. So yeah...you need revenue. You kind of need a lot of it. As I'll detail more in a subsequent chapter, I recommend pushing yourself to a sustainable $300,000 a year in your own client revenue before launching out on your own.

So how do you pursue $300,000 a year without pursuing revenue? Isn't setting that goal literally the definition of *pursuing revenue*? Not really. To understand, you need to watch the movie *Remember the Titans* with Denzel Washington. It's a football movie, and actually, what I'm about to write would probably be true of just about any football movie, but I like Denzel, and I love *Remember the Titans*. The movie is set in an era in the United States when racial segregation was at its peak. To combat it, states were beginning to bus black students to white schools to force integration. Predictably, it created some tension. Then Denzel Washington steps on to the scene, playing the character of Coach Herman Boone. He was hired as the new head coach of the state champion Titans, and In case you've never seen a Denzel Washington movie before, he's not white. Needless to say, the white coaching staff was less than excited about this new non-white football coach, and one of the more embarrassing eras of our nation's history is depicted in what I assume to be painful accuracy.

When you read reviews of *Remember the Titans*, they never discuss the amazing footage of passes being completed or touchdowns being scored. We don't read anything about the quality hits from the defense. I've never seen a single review even mention anything involved in actually playing football. Why? Wasn't this a football movie after all? The reason is simple. This isn't, in fact, a football movie; it's a movie about counting lives changed. When you go solo, your revenue is the touchdown, the pass completed, the field goal. It's exciting. If you're going to win a football game, you need touchdowns and passes completed and field goals, but that's just the score. That's just the revenue. What really counts is the lives changed.

In the movie, the impact comes from the scene where Coach Boone takes these racially mixed group of kids to the point of exhaustion on a run that ends at a Civil War battlefield, where American's spilled their blood to fight a war that was mostly about race. The impact of the movie is felt when a white student finally extends an arm to shake the hand of a star black player.

We love this movie because the points scored are exciting. The music gets us ramped up. The blistering defensive hits. The Hail Mary passes. The runs. The touchdowns. The points, the revenue, is exciting, and the movie needs it. As much as we need that higher calling message, it doesn't impact the same without being delivered in a package of exciting football action. Revenue is fun. Revenue is exciting, but revenue, in the end, is not what we remember; we remember the lives we've changed.

In my practice, one of the things I offer for free is to help clients who are struggling with a crippling debt crisis. I don't file bankruptcy for anyone. I don't know how. Remember the whole "I don't even know where the courtrooms are" thing? So I don't do bankruptcy, but I've been through my own debt crisis. My wife and I racked up a truly ridiculous amount of debt and then added a huge student loan on top of it. We weren't getting sued by anyone, but we were in trouble. We were paying our mortgage late, robbing Peter to pay Paul every month. We weren't even living paycheck to paycheck. It was worse than that. But then, someone stepped in and helped us. They didn't give us any money, but they set us on the right track and got our heads screwed on straight for the first time in our marriage. We genuinely turned our lives around, stopped borrowing money and paid off debt that was way up into the six figures (way, way up). In response, I help people in the same situation. I coach them through the budgeting. I spend a lot of time on the phone, building their confidence back up. I even toss in the occasional lawyerly advice about how to tell their creditors to stick it where the sun doesn't shine. Sure, the creditors will get paid but in a way that allows my client's family to regain their financial, emotional, and spiritual health.

How much do I charge? I charge the same as the person who helped us when we needed it: not a single dime. This can be time-consuming work, but it's worth it when you measure your success by lives changed as opposed to revenue. I literally get to see people transition from scared and terrified, ready to give up, and bring them back to the power and confidence that God designed them to have. To say that this is satisfying is an understatement; I love it.

So that's great. I donate some of my time to a worthy cause that helps people, and it changes lives. That doesn't pay any bills though. Still, I strongly believe that your mission to change lives should not be limited to the occasional pro bono project; you need to infuse your entire practice with the mission of changing lives and measure that success.

For my particular area of the law, I'm not delivering battered women from their oppressive husbands by handling their divorce. I'm not winning judgments to families injured in serious car accidents so they can pay their medical bills and heal. I'm a transactional lawyer. I draft contracts and negotiate leases and restructure companies, and to be honest, I'm pretty good at it. But am I changing lives? I really enjoy this work. As crazy as it sounds, I love knocking out a really good operating agreement for a limited liability company. The stuff everyone hates, the boring stuff that makes your eyes roll back in your head, I love that stuff. Still, am I changing lives? I needed to rethink what I was delivering, and the root of all of it was in the exceptionally boring nature of the work I do (unless you're a huge nerd like me that doesn't think it's boring). The more I thought about it, I wasn't delivering documents; I was delivering peace of mind and security.

I deliver peace of mind by handling these mundane and boring projects to clients who absolutely don't care about the words, the pages, and pages of words that I've written. They have peace because they know that I have their back. I hear this from clients all the time. "I'm glad you handled this because I know you've got my back." My clients know 100 percent without a doubt that I only care about one thing: ensuring that their documents are well drafted, and that they accomplish their goal.

The goal of delivering peace of mind is directly related to the goal of delivering security. We live in a world where the work that I do can be considered something of a commodity. I can draft an operating agreement for you, or you can download one from the Internet. The deliverable, in terms of words on the page, is pretty much the same, but the document you're getting from the Internet, or from the attorney down the street who honestly doesn't care about your case a whole lot more than the Internet does, has nothing to do with your specific life; and the problem is that you're not going to know it until there is a dispute, when it's too late to fix it.

What I deliver is the knowledge that I've spent time getting to know you, getting to know what's going on with your family, what your relationship is like with your business partner, your employees. I know about the products and services you offer, your vendors, your revenue, your expenses. I know what you are confident about and what you are worried about, and for heaven's sakes, I don't accomplish any of this with a cute little questionnaire that you fill out and send over to me. God bless, I hate those. There is nothing more impersonal than telling a client how much you care about their life and then sending them a form to fill out because you're not willing to have a simple conversation with them like a normal human being.

I've had other attorneys express surprise at how much I know about my clients. There is no magic formula. I just spend a lot of time talking to my clients. I'm a small business nerd. So spending time talking to small business owners is a pretty cool way to spend my time, and when I talk to clients, I spend a little time telling them about me too. That I've owned a few businesses and held management positions in corporate America. I have kids. I adopt dogs. I live in a nice suburb of Chicago. I like biking. I don't go through all of this with every client; I just talk to them the way normal people have conversations, and we learn a lot about each other. Then I take what I've learned, and I put together documents that solve their problems.

I design documents to avoid the things they are worried about. I look at the things that they love; and I look into the future to see how those things can be affected, damaged, destroyed. Then I draft documents to avoid those problems. I look at their relationship with their partners and employees and filter it through my experience dealing with people for almost five decades of life and anticipate problems and draft documents to avoid those problems or at least provide a means to resolve those problems if things do go wrong.

Suddenly, sitting at a laptop and drafting operating agreements doesn't sound so lifeless. Suddenly it seems like there is most certainly a way that I can measure lives changed as opposed to revenue generated. Because of the work I do, my clients can focus on driving their business instead of fighting with each other because the drive-through lawyer they had draft their documents didn't see that they needed a third member to their board of directors because they were likely to fight about major issues. They can focus on delivering for their customers as opposed to arguing over how to get cash into the business because I saw that they'd need cash and built three different mechanisms to get it into their shareholder agreement. So they can just execute on those mechanisms, bring in cash, and not fight about how pissed off they are at each other because one has cash to put in and the other doesn't.

The simplest way I put this is that I keep my clients out of court. Even litigators, who earn their living in courtrooms, will tell you that going to court is always some level of coin toss. I can measure my success by the number of my clients who never go to court, or avoid pitfalls of business partnership, or build their business to a point where it can be sold for enough money to let them retire at fifty years old. Suddenly, looking at my practice this way, my ability to measure lives changed is incredible. And trust me, if I can do this with an industry as boring as transactional corporate law, you can definitely find a way to measure lives changed in your practice as well.

One of my favorite clients is V. V is a software engineer. His story could be a book entirely by itself. Incredible immigration story. But staying on focus, V designs mobile apps. So he's not really changing any lives, right? V took his normally boring day job and designed an app that helps police officers deal with emotional problems without the stigma of going to see a traditional therapist. He accomplished this with software. Lives changed.

Another client, and good friend, does roofing. Yes, he changes people lives by ensuring that they don't get rained on, but in his spare time, he goes into the deepest jungles in Central and South America and uses his construction skills to build schools. Lives changed.

Take some time to think about what is really at the heart of what you do for a living. Of course, what you do all day needs to be related to revenue; if not, you can't pay your mortgage. But go a layer deeper. How can you rethink your practice to measure lives changed as opposed to revenue generated? When you do, and when you execute on that goal of lives changed, you can count on one thing: the revenue will come.

I would love to tell you that my success in going solo is exclusively the result of my genius marketing and business planning skills, but that's not true. I don't want to slip into the mystical here, but I am firmly convinced that much of my success comes to me because of my dedication to changing lives both in and outside the office. The desire to change lives needs to permeate your time outside the office just as much, if not more, than your time at the office. The world has a way of taking care of you if you dedicate yourself to taking care of it. In addition to sorting out all of the things you need to get done to start your own office, think about the things you can do in the office and otherwise to genuinely make an impact on people's lives. However, do it with a giving heart, and never keep score. Just keep pouring good into the world, and watch what the world does in return. You'll probably be surprised.

QUITTING YOUR JOB

You've read this far, and you're ramped up. You love the idea of freedom. You're building your vision of what your life will look like when you go solo. You're comfortable in your own skin so you can engage in real sales. You've defined what it means to measure lives changed instead of just pursing a pile of cash. The time has come to quit your job, but I know from personal experience that there is a right and wrong way to do that.

This book is all about me quitting my job. I actually quit two jobs in order to go solo. The nice downtown job I walked out on was my second job as an attorney. I was only there for a year, and it became obvious that these were very nice people, but they didn't really need me, and I didn't really need them. I quit another longer-term gig before going downtown. I was with a strong, fast-growing multi-practice law firm in the suburbs of Chicago for eleven years.

The good news is that you have two examples to learn from: when I left my swanky downtown job with the view of the Chicago River, I did it right; and when I left the job before that, I did it wrong. Very wrong. There are some solid takeaways from both experiences. Let's be honest, it's far more interesting to talk about the one that I screwed up, so let's start there.

Quitting…the Wrong Way

I had been with this firm for eleven years. As I've discussed elsewhere in this book, I was never a rock star when it came to billable hours. For an attorney, a hundred billable hours a month is pretty pathetic. So I can proudly say that I was slightly better than pathetic my entire career at this suburban firm. The main boss, the founder of the firm, liked me, and at first, he was the only boss. He owned the firm, had no partners, and the buck stopped with him. I did a lot of work directly for him, and the other attorneys in the firm gave me projects as well. At first, I even went to court, but it didn't take them long to realize that courtroom work wasn't my special gift. The skills that rose to the top for me were transactional. I could draft documents well, and I was good at communicating with clients. While my work was usually good, I tended to deliver projects slow, often blowing deadlines. I was not responsive enough with clients, sometimes taking days to return a phone call or e-mail.

One thing I was good at was bringing in business. In addition to bringing in my own clients, I was often called into initial client meetings to close the deal and get the clients to sign. I had eleven years of sales in my background. So for me, knocking down new business was just second nature, and obviously, any firm is going to appreciate someone who can bring in a good amount of new business. However, my billing was so low that it created tension. This became exaggerated when the founder brought on partners. He had always been in my corner and was patient with my low hours. He even took me to lunch a few times to have an honest conversation about my hours and why they were so low. He was genuinely trying to help. His partners later, however, were less interested in helping, and it's not third grade.

I had no reasonable expectation that the partners in my law firm were there to help me work. Yes, they were there to help me develop management skills and leadership qualities and legal skills and the ability to work on higher and higher level projects, but they weren't really there to help me learn to strap my ass to my chair and just bill hours. Keep in mind that the firm was looking for six billable hours per day. That's exceptionally reasonable. Still, I was blowing it. I wasn't even billing six hours a day.

So that's a long way of getting to this simple point: I was developing tension with the new managing partner. The founder has stepped down as part of a long-term succession plan. He was still in the office every day but had officially turned the management of the firm over to a new managing partner. This new managing partner and I didn't have outright conflict, but we never really clicked on a personal level like I had with the founder of the firm. He didn't hate me, but he wasn't cutting me any slack either. He expected results, and for what they were paying me, that was fair.

This tension led to a series of things happening. I was delayed one year from being officially put on partnership track. At that firm, we didn't use the term *junior partner*, but there was a role that was basically that. You would sit in on the partner meetings and start to see the inner workings of the firm. I was eligible to be put on this partnership track after a certain number of years with the firm, but at my annual review, they delayed me one year because my hours were too low. So I busted it the next year and got my hours up to a level that was almost respectable for a suburban law firm, and they put on partnership track. They even included me in the annual partnership retreat for a weekend of in-depth planning and discussion of where the firm was going and how it was going to get there. But then, several months later, I was asked to come into a meeting with the new managing partner and another partner who was basically his unofficial second in command. They informed me that I was being pulled off of the partnership track again. My hours were too low. This time, that really fired me up. I knew I wasn't killing it on hours, but I also felt like I was at least keeping pace with the other attorneys who were either partners or on the partnership track. So I checked. Our billing system allowed me to look at how many hours everyone was billing, so I ran an analysis. I was the second highest biller out of all of the partners or people on partnership track. I was pissed.

I spent literally the rest of my day writing and rewriting an e-mail to the new management partner, asking for an explanation. Why is the second highest biller being pulled from partnership track for having low billable hours? I was bringing in dramatically more business than anyone else on the partnership team or partnership track. The next best rainmaker after me brought in less than half of my originations. I did my best to explain this in a professional manner. I hope I was professional, but at I know that my frustration came ringing through in that e-mail, and the response served one single purpose: it absolutely solidified my decision to leave the firm. The simple response was that my originations were so high that it didn't make sense that my billable hours were so low.

The following day, the entire firm lost access to the section of the billing software that allowed me to look up everyone else's billables and originations, and I was reminded that I had received a substantial raise when I was put on the partnership track, but they had graciously not taken back that raise when I was bumped off the partnership track.

I read that e-mail several times and was finally able to come to terms with it. I put my resume together and started calling recruiters that afternoon. I was out.

Interviewing went well, and the recruiter I worked with did a great job. I had three interviews, and all three firms were expressing interest. I received an offer right way from one of the firms that actually extended the offer during my initial interview. The other firms wanted follow-ups, and eventually I received an offer from a great firm, the one with the great view of the Chicago River. They brought me right away as a partner. Not an equity partner yet—I wasn't putting down cash to buy in—but I'd have *partner* on my letterhead and my e-mail signature. I was happy, and these all seemed like genuinely good people (and they were).

So I needed to quit my job, and I did it so poorly that it actually merits a chapter in a book about going solo. The primary mistake I made was entering into the process of resigning through anger. It's ironic; I had counselled a hundred clients on the importance of not making major life changes while in an emotional state, but here I was with a good downtown law firm respecting my abilities as an attorney, and I had a chance to stick it to these guys who had bumped me off of partnership track *twice*. This was my moment. As it turns out, it was my moment to act like a spoiled brat.

In addition to acting while angry, I also succumbed to pressure from the new firm to make a mad grab for clients. We constructed a timeline for my resignation that would ensure that I had the ability to reach out to as many clients as possible as quickly as possible. They pressured me to give notice at 10:00 a.m. on a Friday, effective that day, literally giving same-day notice, but then, I would give a week of transition after that if the firm wanted me to do so. However, at the end of the day, this was me walking in and saying to the new managing partner, "I quit…effective today."

Let's get something perfectly clear as you start making plans to go solo: don't ever give same-day notice. We don't need to get into the intricacies of whether it's ethical or right or justifiable; let's all just agree right now that giving same-day notice is an asshole move. Don't ever do it.

The main mistake I made was that I caved to the pressure from the new firm to give short notice. I think they were envisioning a very *Jerry Maguire* moment where my old firm would rush to their phones to try to secure clients and I would rush to my phone to try to secure clients, and it would be very dramatic. But it wasn't very dramatic. I sent letters to all of the clients I had worked with (more on that below), and some of them called me and some of them didn't. It was pretty low key.

In a great fit of irony, about a year later, I was at my new firm downtown, and they were bringing in another new attorney. As the managing partner was introducing him to me, the topic of giving notice came up, and my new managing partner told this guy, "In terms of how much notice to give, just do what you think is right." Wow! Where was this sage advice when I was dropping my same-day-notice bomb at their insistence? Regardless, at the end of it all, it's on me. I went against my gut and pulled an asshole move. Don't make that same mistake. Give an amount of notice that is fair to both you and your employer. Simple enough.

Don't worry, there are more mistakes to learn from. I'll get into more details about this in an entire chapter dedicated to bringing clients with you. However, I stretched the concept of who I should send my announcement letters to. In the legal industry, the way this normally works is that you quit your job and send letters out to clients you've worked with to let them know you're moving to a new firm. Then those clients have the opportunity to either come with you or stay at the firm you're leaving. It's pretty simple, actually. In the legal industry, there are some rules about what you can write in your letter (don't bash your former employer, etc.), and there are some rules about who you can send those letters to. You can't just send letters to every client of the firm and cross your fingers; you can only send letters to clients that you've established a professional relationship with.

I took that concept and stretched it. I did not send letters out to *every client* of the firm. I genuinely had established at least some kind of working relationship with every client who received a letter from me, but being completely honest, some of these letters shouldn't have gone out. My main mistake was that I sent letters to clients that I had not brought into the firm. These were other attorneys' clients. Don't do that. Later, there is an entire chapter about securing clients and ensuring that your clients go with you when you leave, but that chapter pertains 100 percent to your clients. The clients you brought into the firm.

It was a mistake for me to reach out to clients who had been originated by other attorneys. I was well within the rules of professional conduct, but do us all a favor, and don't allow the bare minimum of rules to be your guide as to how to conduct yourself; you can't build a business as a solo if you're constantly operating just within the definition of what is wrong.

There is a popular phrase, "Do stupid things, get stupid prizes." So what stupid prize did I get for these two mistakes? In exchange for giving same-day notice and stretching the limit of who I should have sent letters to, I received a cease and desist letter from my old firm. Well, technically I didn't receive it. My old firm wrote the cease and desist letter, went on my new firm's website, and got a list of every partner at my new firm; and, you guessed it, they sent that cease and desist letter to every single partner at that new firm. It was a third grade move made out of anger that was grossly beneath the founding partner of my old firm. They issued a crappy response to my crappy exit. And just like me, they stretched the ethical limits of our industry when they did it. They even included a suggestion that the reason I didn't become a partner at their firm was because I lacked the funds to buy in.[5] There is no rational reason for them to

---

[5] Technically, this was true. As soon as I got bumped off the partnership track for the second time, I used my buy-in fund that I had been stockpiling to pay down

include this allegation in the letter other than to try to embarrass me. It helped me to fully come to terms with the fact that I was right to leave that firm but it caused me plenty of sleepless nights as well and was entirely unnecessary.

The takeaway here is that I could have avoided all of this by refraining from my two main mistakes. First, that letter would never have been sent if I hadn't given same-day notice, and it would never have been sent if I had limited my announcement letters to those clients I had personally brought into my old firm. In exchange, I earned myself and my new partners a massive waste of time with a brief letter writing war that resulted in little more than each side blowing off steam that had built up over the course of many months.

Quitting…Improved

My next resignation went better, in no small part, because of the lessons I had learned from round one. I knew that I wanted to give adequate notice and only send announcement letters to clients I had brought into the firm myself. No poaching. I decided that I would offer a short notice period mainly because I felt like I was a bit of a drain on their finances. I was being paid well and was still clocking in with my famously low billable hours. So they weren't making a ton of money off me. I thought it was actually somewhat likely that they would be relieved to see me go and anxious to get me off the payroll. I stepped into my managing partner's office on a Tuesday and offered to have that coming Friday be my last day. I also made it perfectly clear, both verbally and in my resignation letter, that I could stay for a longer transition time if they wanted me to.

My managing partner's reaction will stay with me forever. He is one of the most genuinely decent people you will ever meet. He said to me with a tone of genuine concern, "You don't need a firm?" That's the last thing I was expecting him to say. I thought he might be angry, perhaps he'd try to get me to stay, argue about whether I'd be taking clients, etc.; but instead, he expressed genuine concern over

---

other debt instead.

whether or not I needed a firm around me in order to function as an attorney. This is a critical observation. I wasn't going out on my own because this was a bad place; I was going out on my own because I was simply wired up in a way that didn't contribute a whole lot to the firm I was with, and they didn't contribute a whole lot to me, and that's okay.

My answer to his question, if being honest, was that I hadn't actually had a firm for several months. I had essentially weaned myself off using any support staff. I had stopped giving work to other attorneys (unless it was outside my area of practice), and from day one, I had never really received any work from other attorneys, just a small handful of projects over the course of a little over a year. So the immediate answer to the question was, "No, I don't need a law firm." I didn't say it that way. These were attorneys who had been practicing for decades with a firm that had existed since the 1940s. I wasn't about to tell them that I had cracked the code, and their entire business model was useless.

With my resignation complete, I had to send out letters to my clients to let them know I was changing firms. Again. This gave me a bit of heartburn. I needed to convey two things in this letter. First, that as a client, they could trust me to be a wise advisor who could help them make good decisions and avoid costly mistakes. "Oh, and by the way, remember when I told you a year ago that I was switching firms? Yeah, well, I'm kinda switching firms again, but trust me, this time, it's definitely the right move."

I needed to convey confidence in the letter announcing this second move. So I decided to highlight that I was heading out on my own so that I could practice law the way I had always wanted to with a genuine focus on how much I love small business. The letter was a success. I took every single one of my clients with me; not a single client stayed behind. I did field a few phone calls, asking why I was moving again and whether this really was my final move, or could I possibly be moving again soon? I handled those calls well, put my clients' minds at ease, and started working for them almost as though nothing had happened.

The best part about this second resignation was that it was peaceful. I hadn't done anything to motivate anyone to deem me their enemy. No cease and desist letters this time, and I made a promise when I left that downtown firm. I told them that I would continue to refer as much work to them as possible. They were very good at what they did, particularly in the areas of estate planning and real estate tax appeals. I've remained true to my word. I send them at least a couple of new clients every month, and plan to continue to do so.

Please don't limit your reading of this chapter to the two mistakes I made. Of course I would like you to give adequate notice and market only to the clients you brought into your firm before you left. These are important details, but the larger and more critical takeaway is that I acted outside of what my gut was telling me was right because I was angry. I think I was right to be angry, but having a good reason to be upset is not a justification to act on those feelings. Do what is right regardless of how upset you may be at your current employer. However, this is difficult to do in the heat of the moment. So be deliberate about designing the plan you will use when you resign, and take your time. Don't throw it together in a week. Start thinking about this weeks or months ahead of time, and seek out the advice of trusted mentors.

I have great respect for a mentor of mine who is also a close friend, and before I gave my same-day resignation, he said to me, "Wow, that doesn't seem right. Honestly, that doesn't seem like you. That's not cool." He was right. However, by the time I went to him to tell him what was going on, my emotions were in full swing, and I had convinced myself that I was handling this the right way. Or perhaps it would be more fair that I was dedicated to *giving them what they deserved*, which is a childish way to end an eleven-year employment relationship.

In the legal industry, we have specific rules on how these resignations work. Perhaps you have similar rules, or perhaps you have none. Perhaps there is no rule at all about who you can market to once you leave. So why not shoot a letter or e-mail out to every single client of the firm you're leaving? There is no rule stopping you, right? Let me give you a bit of wisdom that I gained by doing it the wrong way: don't do it. You want to walk out of that office with your head held high and with your employer wishing they could have found a way to keep you. You don't want them tossing rotten tomatoes at your back while you walk out the door. Do the right thing, follow your gut, and listen to that little voice in your head or your mentor who's telling you that you're being an asshole.

One of my great regrets in the way I left my first firm, the one in the suburbs, was that I allowed a personal spat between me and the managing partner to permanently end great relationships I had formed with great people. I had good friends at that firm who I have never talked to since. I had an incredible mentor in the founder of that firm that I could be learning from even today, and with my low billing numbers, I could probably have made a graceful exit that made everyone happy and maintained all of those relationships. They'd be sad to see my revenue leave, but they'd be happy to no longer see my lackluster monthly billing numbers. I think it would have been okay. Also, professionally, I have lost the ability to refer clients to some of the best estate planning, litigation, and commercial real estate attorneys I've ever met. That's one hell of a high price to pay for the extremely brief satisfaction of *sticking it to them* with a same-day resignation.

Learn from my mistakes, and give yourself the peace of mind and clear focus that you can only get from a properly handled resignation. You have a big job to do: you need to secure all of your clients under your own roof. The way you reach out to them after you resign is critical but even more important is the way you interact with those clients in the year leading up to that resignation. Let's dive into that.

BRINGING CLIENTS
WITH YOU

The theme of this book is planning a strategy to go on your own well in advance of doing so. We are not leaving a job and walking into the abyss of the unknown. Quite the opposite. Instead we're putting a detailed plan into place and ensuring success months or years before you go on your own so that you're riding a wave of success into your solo career as opposed to trying to create success after you've quit your job. This is a guide to put all of your pieces in place on the chess board and then make your final move when you know the timing is right. Calling out checkmate at the end of game of chess is only dramatic because you made all the right moves leading up it. So set aside the impulse to relentlessly pursue your dreams, and act today because there is no tomorrow. There definitely is a tomorrow, and tomorrow, you're going to want to have some clients to work with. So let's be smart about this, and build up a book of business, and then do all of the right things to ensure that book goes with you when you leave.

We're securing two things: first, your book of business you're taking with you, and second, your ability to generate new business as well. We covered the ability to generate new business already, and it's critical. In this chapter, we'll discuss the importance of bringing the clients you already have with you when you leave. Securing a book of business that you can bring with you when you go solo is probably the most important step in going out on your own. It's critical that you convince the clients you brought into your current job to follow you when you leave.

This concept is almost always surprising to people outside the legal industry. Everyone assumes, lawyers, being the type of people they are, that every lawyer has a fifty-eight-page employment agreement with an extremely onerous, noncompete clause that allows your employer you willfully destroy your life if you even think about contacting any clients after you go solo, but that's just not accurate. Having any kind of a noncompete as an attorney is actually quite rare. Even attorneys who have made partner will usually take their clients with them if the partnership breaks up.

One attorney I know who went solo was a victim of this exact scenario. Sean didn't choose to go solo. He had been working hard at a firm handling litigation matters and a fair amount of residential real estate closings, and things seemed to be going fairly well. There were the occasional storm clouds when the partners would flair up at one another, but that's normal. We're lawyers after all; we like to argue about things. However, on a Monday morning, without any official warning whatsoever, Sean read the e-mail that changed his life: "The firm is closing permanently on Friday. Have a nice day." I'm paraphrasing, of course, but that was the message. "Happy Monday. You're all fired as of Friday." The partnership had split up, and the main partners were going their separate ways, taking their clients with them. So Sean was out of a job with five days to figure out what he was going to do.

Sean undertook the task of going solo with five days' notice, and I've never once heard him complain about it. I took about three years to get myself ready to go out on my own. Sean is making it on his own, and I've had the pleasure of subbing out some work to him, and it's no wonder why he's building a good practice. He's a good lawyer, but more importantly, he's a good man. Let's be inspired by Sean, without exactly following in his footsteps. I'd rather see everyone reading this book walk into the solo life with a little more time spent putting the pieces into place (an option that Sean didn't have).[6]

---

[6] Sean's case is another solid example of why going solo makes sense for the right person. The main reason people tend to stay in their jobs is because they have "job security." There is no job security. You have job security until you don't. That may sound cynical, but ask Sean if I'm right. We'll add that to the reasons

You need to know how much of a book of business to build before you go solo. The first question you need to ask yourself is how much income is enough when you are on your own. The amount most firms want you to bill for them every year is far more than the average person needs to live on. Most attorneys can live very comfortably on the number of hours they were regularly billing at their jobs. The firm I originally worked for asked for six billable hours per day. That's a fairly low requirement. But even at that low number, at my billing rate, that was about $1,800 per day. This adds up to about $450,000 per year. That would be a great income! I could definitely squeak by on $450,000 a year. Heck, I don't even need that much. I have mentioned a goal of $300,000 in previous chapters, and I think that's the right number for most people. It's a solid income that is large enough to motivate you to put in the hard work that is required when you go solo, and it's enough revenue that you still have a very comfortable living after paying all of the expenses involved in going solo.

Set your own number. However, if you are struggling to decide how much income you need, just start with $300,000. Don't overthink it. If you hit that number, you'll be fine. You can lower the goal later to allow for a bit more family time if you like, or push it higher if the kids are starting college soon and you need some extra cash. Whatever your number is starting out, we now reverse engineer that number, and you start building your own little mini-practice within your current firm in the months or years leading up to your move to go solo.

You're not going to quit your job until you have a solid and very consistent book of annual business from your own clients that is at least the $300,000 you need (or whatever number you choose) every year with great consistency. The last thing you want to do is grab a client that has a huge project, generating a huge amount of billable hours that puts you over the top for your annual $300,000 goal. Then you quit! But that was not a book of business; It was a proj-

---

to consider going solo. Ask yourself if the job security you are clinging to is actually real.

ect. One project, to be exact. You cannot quit your job until you've achieved a level of monthly and annual consistency in your book of business that confirms as much as possible that it will continue after you've gone solo.

For me, I had been running at least a $300,000 book of business for two years before I left my first job. I was then able to continue that level at my new job downtown. So I had at least three steady years of strong consistency before going out on my own. I simply wouldn't have done so without that consistency. The combination of generating new business and establishing long-term strong relationships with clients that had consistent monthly needs was well established before I made the jump into solo practice.

I can imagine in my mind my former employers reading this and their blood boiling a bit. "He brought all these clients into the firm knowing at the time that he would be leaving and taking them with him." Well, not exactly. It's true that I had thought many times about leaving my first firm, but I wasn't bringing clients into that practice knowing at the time that I would leave. I dreamed about leaving from time to time, but it was never a solid plan until I started to tangle with the newly appointed managing partner. By then, my book of business was already fairly solid, and the reason I went to another firm is that I simply lacked the confidence to go out on my own at that time. I actually think that the process of bringing all of my clients with me to my new firm helped me (ironically) to build that confidence to do it again at some point in the future. When I eventually came to the realization that I didn't need a firm around me in order to succeed, I was confident in both aspects of my book of business (the base of existing clients plus the consistency in bringing in new clients).

I encourage you to avoid the mindset that bringing in all of these clients and planning to take them all with you when you leave is somehow sinister. Bear in mind that your current firm is going to make plenty of money off these clients while you're still working there, and they have a fair shot at keeping them when you leave (but we'll do our best to avoid that). Also, never forget Sean's example. Your firm has the absolute ability to pull the rug out from under you and let you go whenever they like, and if they do, they'll still take a shot at grabbing your clients from you as you walk out the door. This is the nature of employment. If both sides are not gaining enough benefit, then one of the sides can simply terminate the relationship. That might be you, or it might be your employer. So don't feel bad at all about bringing clients into your firm right now even knowing that you may be leaving at some point and taking them with you. If your firm doesn't present enough value to you to keep you interested in working there, then your departure is their responsibility, not yours. In exactly the same way, if you stop delivering value to your employer, you can expect them to cut you loose in exactly the same way. As the saying goes, business is business. Your freedom and your income are at stake. Don't allow yourself to be drawn into a false sense of loyalty that your employer probably doesn't share.

As I've mentioned several times, I was never a star when it came to billable hours at my first firm, and I always had the feeling that the founding partner of the firm was exceptionally loyal to me. As he brought on more partners, I often suspected that he was consistently defending me behind closed doors, arguing my case before his other partners. However, as the firm shifted into the control of a new managing partner as part of a well-planned succession strategy, my perception of loyalty began to evaporate. The nail in the coffin was the comment that I received when I objected to being removed from the management team for the second time despite having stronger billing numbers than the other members of that team. "When we added you to the management team, we gave you a significant increase in salary. When we removed you from the team, we didn't scale that increase back." This veiled threat to cut my salary was the confirmation I needed to know that any whisper of loyalty toward me was gone, and I was gone within sixty days of that e-mail.

You never know when your last day will be, and it's only fair that your employer never really knows when you might decide to go solo. So go ahead and build your book of business, and perfect the craft of generating a consistent flow of new clients so that if the day comes that you lose confidence in the stability of your job, you'll have the option just make your own job and go solo.

You May Need an Interim Step

Until now, we've been operating under the assumption that every law firm, or any other type of service firm, not only allows its employees to market and network but actually encourages it. This raises an interesting question that I had never considered when I started writing this book. What if your firm doesn't let you market and bring in clients? Honestly, this never occurred to me until I started interviewing attorneys in the process of writing this book. I also have had conversations with a few attorneys I thought about hiring along the way, and they said that their bosses just needed them to do the work they assigned, and they didn't want them out there networking and bringing in business.

This was shocking to me. I am a sales guy down to my bone marrow, so the thought of a law office that didn't want everyone out there selling was bizarre to me. However, it's actually pretty common. So what do you do if you're in a situation where the firm you are working for doesn't let you market? They won't let you attend networking events. They don't let you join the Chamber of Commerce. They don't even want you posting on LinkedIn.

I hate to be blunt, but I think there is only one solution: you need to start looking for a new job. I know that sounds a little extreme, but I don't see any way around it. Having a solid book of business that you can bring with you when you go solo is absolutely critical to your success. The only other option is to build up a massive savings, and pray that it lasts until you can get rolling on your own. I know that sounds like a brutal way to step out into the world of solo practice.

Your only other option would be to do your best to lure away clients from the other attorneys in your firm, and that is not something I recommend (more on that below). I strongly believe that you should only seek to bring along those clients who you personally brought into the firm, not the clients you did a lot of work for; that's too broad. I only recommend taking with you those clients that you personally brought into the firm. This is one of the things that I got right. I never took a single client with me that brought with them a feeling that I'd done something wrong. Of all of my clients, I only took one that was originated by another attorney, and he specifically asked me to do so.

The last thing you need when you're starting out on your own is the feeling that you need to be constantly looking over your shoulder because you've stretched the boundaries of right and wrong. Or look at it this way: you're in the middle of building your book of business, and you're working hard at it. You're building strong relationships, you're spending time networking and marketing, and some guy down the hall leaves the firm and takes your client with him just because you assigned a few projects to him. If you don't like the sound of that, then don't do that to anyone else either. Only take clients that you personally brought into the firm. Keep this aspect of your life simple. You'll have plenty of other things to worry about as a solo.

If the number of clients you have to take with you is zero because you're not allowed to market, then you really need to look at joining a new firm that lets you spread your wings a little. The pitch you would make while interviewing at news firms is easy. "I'm doing good work at the firm I'm with now, but I'd really like to spread my wings and generate my own business and bring in my own clients." This is a line that many law firms or other professional service firms would love to hear during an interview. They very thing you're not allowed to do at your current firm might be just the reason someone hires you for your next job.

Also, keep an open mind about this new firm. I want you to consider going solo because I love the freedom and income I've been able to enjoy on my own, but you might love this new firm. You might have freedom that you hadn't expected. You might be genuinely fulfilled and have time to spend with your family, etc. Not every firm out there is a dark oppressive factory of grim daily life. You might just love this new job. So if you make the bold move of switching jobs so you can start to market, then keep your mind 100 percent open to staying at that new job for good. You never know; things might be great. I always tell my clients to keep their options open. Give this new job an honest chance. With that mindset, you're not genuinely getting this new job for the sole purpose of walking out with your clients at some point in the future. Be open to the possibilities this new firm presents.

Remember, too, that transitioning quickly from a new job to going solo isn't entirely easy. In my case, I left my job of ten years and went to a new firm downtown. All of my clients eventually came with me, except for one who had a litigation matter underway, and it would not have made sense to switch firms. A little over a year later, I was contacting all of those clients again and telling them I've gone out on my own. Many of them congratulated me, as noted earlier, but many of them also reacted with a touch of coolness. They must have been thinking, "Is this guy okay? Two moves in about a year. Is he reliable?" Keeping all of my clients the second time I moved was harder than the first.

If you're going to switch to a new firm that will let you market, then plan to be there for a few years. We're putting chess pieces into place, and chess is a slow-moving game; we're not diving off a cliff. For me, moving twice within a year was a challenge I probably could have done well to avoid. Plan to give this some time out of fairness to your new employer and to make the second transition of your clients (if needed) smoother and more reliable.

Once you've started bringing in your own business, whether that's at your existing firm or a new one that lets you market, the rest of this chapter assumes that you've decided to make the jump and go solo. In the legal industry, attorneys are not allowed to contact their clients before they leave in order to secure their commitment to stay with them. This adds an element of pressure to your move, but it's actually a good kind of pressure. It puts you in the position of maximum risk. You need to walk out on your own, and *then* reach out to your clients to tell them you've opened your own shop. If you haven't laid the foundation of a strong relationship with each of those clients, you're going to have a few sleepless nights wondering who is coming with you and who is not.

What can you do to essentially ensure your clients will come with you? I can only tell you what my clients have told me when they made the first switch to my downtown firm and then the second switch a year later when I went solo. Many were surprised that I asked at all. "Well, yeah, I'm coming with you. You're my lawyer."

My nature is to spend a lot of time forming personal relationships with my clients. A lot of attorneys will tell you this is a bad idea, but I am telling you that this is the key to my success.

These personal connections are something that some law firms really discourage. "Don't get connected personally." I disagree. My first firm was run by a man who was a master at forming tight personal relationships with his clients and delivering great legal services to them at the same time. He was their lawyer, not his firm, or his nice office. The relationship was personal, and that is the key to ensuring that your clients come with you.

One of the tipping points in my decision to go solo was a conversation with a good friend of mine, Don, who had gone solo many years earlier. I mentioned my thoughts about going out on my own, and he was instantly enthusiastic, almost demanding that I do so immediately. I expressed my concern about clients staying with me when I went solo, and his response sticks in my memory to this day: "Call twenty of your clients, and ask them the name of your law firm. None of them will know, because you're their lawyer, not your firm. You." And he was right.

The key to building this personal connection that cannot be broken by going solo is to be your genuine self. If you read this book and decide to invent a version of your personality that is well-suited to keeping clients, you're going to fail hard. Similar to the chapter on how to sell, we are not looking for the appearance of a personal connection; we're looking for a true connection between two people.

The main element of building this personal relationship is time. I tend to bond fairly quickly with people, but the truly solid connection comes over many months at least. It's better to give it many years. Part of this is just practical. In my practice, many of my clients don't need legal services very often. So it will take some time just for enough issues to come up that they are interacting with you at all, much less interacting enough to form a personal bond.

In the interim between those lulls when your client doesn't need anything, reach out by phone or e-mail every once in a while. If you reach out by phone for no specific reason, be sure you mention that when you call. I would normally call a little after hours in the hopes of getting the client's voice mail so I could leave a message. Getting a phone call from a lawyer can be a nerve-racking thing. It usually means something bad has happened. So don't give your client heartburn; open up immediately by letting them know you're just checking in. "Hi, it's Jim, your lawyer. No specific reason for calling. No bad news to report. I was just checking in to see how things were going with the new project we worked on putting into place." Something like that. It needs to be extremely obvious that you're just making a friendly call, and you have no bad news to report.

These random check-in calls are a big part of why my clients moved with me. Moreover, when I called and asked how things were going, I was genuinely interested in hearing what they had to say. As a solo, you will have the time to really get to know your clients. So start laying that foundation early and take a few minutes each weak to touch base with clients for nonbusiness issues.

I know my client V is from India. I know he moved here with his wife many years ago, and they actually lived in separate states, far apart from one another to make ends meet when they first came to this country from India. I know they had a small son. I know all of this because I had taken the time over the years to talk to V about his life in addition to just handling his legal matters.

I know my client T is married, never had kids, has his dad living with him, which he loves. I know his dad too, and I can understand why T loves having his dad live with him. He's a fun guy to be around. I know that T used to like going to the wrong kind of bars a little too often, and I know that he and his wife truly love their rescue dogs (even the one missing a leg). I know T can grill up a mean steak, and he likes nice cars.

My point in telling you these things is that I know my clients personally better than most attorneys know their clients. I really love connecting with my clients on this personal level, and I've been told by some very experienced attorneys that it's a mistake, and honestly, I don't care. I like practicing law this way. I like connecting with my clients, and my clients appreciate knowing that I'm someone they can trust, and that I'll never judge them. I've made too many mistakes myself to sit on a throne of judgment on anyone else, and my closest clients know that too.

There is a part of me that loves getting the call even when there is literally nothing that I can do to help a client. Or at the very least, my role will be limited to bringing in an attorney who is able to help them, but generally, they don't want to be handed off to that attorney. They prefer to have me held in the middle of the resolution even if I'm not the one carrying the primary load for the legal work. I'm their attorney; I am the one they trust, and when life goes wrong, I am very honored to be the one they call.

The business aspect of this is that there is absolutely no question that these clients are going to be coming with me when I move from one firm to another. They've entrusted me with the most difficult and challenging aspects of their lives, and forming that level of trust is rare and difficult and time-consuming. You're simply never going to get that unless you take the time with clients outside of the strict practice of law and connect with them on a real level, and that can be tough to do in a traditional law firm with billable requirements. There is no benefit to the partners of a firm if their associates bond in this way with their clients. It's more of a liability, which is the main point of this chapter. If you bond with a client in the way I'm suggesting, they'll follow you wherever you go.

But it's important to pause and be clear about what I'm suggesting here. I'm definitely not suggesting that you conjure up the perception that you are bonding with your clients just so that they will go with you if you leave your job. That fails to pass the genuineness test that I described in the chapter on selling. Far from a sales gimmick, I suggesting that you simply need to be the type of person who loves connecting with people; and in my profession, loves connecting with people at times when they very badly need judgment-free compassion and help.

This is one aspect of going solo that really starkly contrasts with working in a traditional law firm. I love this part of my job. I've had to drop everything to immediately retain local counsel to resolve a fairly embarrassing criminal violation for a client. I've had to calm clients struggling with the fear that a mistake they made could lead to their deportation. There are times when there is literally nothing I can do to help a client, but I'll spend time with them to talk them through the difficulty of their current circumstances. Every minute of this is unbillable time. It's unproductive. It fails to achieve the metrics that a traditional law firm has to enforce in order to survive. It's not profitable; but…it's human.

Trust is the highest level of human interaction possible, and I love being there for people. This is why I make myself available for these calls. It's not because it's good for business, but regardless, making yourself available like this does ultimately have the side benefit of creating incredible client loyalty, and very strong client loyalty is a big part of my success as a solo attorney. So just be there for your clients. Be there for anyone who needs you, professionally or otherwise, and don't keep score. Again, it's about changing the lives of those around you. It's not about revenue. Ironically, if you do so, the revenue seems to come all on its own.

Practical Considerations

There are some limitations on your ability to bring clients with you. As noted, for attorneys, we are not allowed to contact our clients until we've already left our job or at least until we've already given notice of our resignation. Add this to the list of reasons that it's ignorant to quit your job on same-day notice. Rules vary from state to state about when you can give notice, but you want to be sure that you're familiar with your local rules. You may have other restrictions such as a confidentiality agreement or a noncompete agreement.

As a transactional attorney, I spend a lot of time dealing with these agreements, and one of the most common statements I hear is that noncompete agreements aren't worth the paper they are written on. It's true that a noncompete can sometimes be difficult to enforce in court. Judges don't like to see people restrained from earning a living, but you shouldn't simply assume that you can violate your noncompete and leave it to the courts to refuse to enforce it.

First and foremost, let's forget about the enforceability for a moment, and remember that this is something you actually agreed to. Don't live your life on the basis of doing whatever you can get away with simply because you assume that a court won't impose consequences. You should honor the agreements you sign. Moreover, I would say that courts invalidate a noncompete agreement *often*, but *often* isn't the same as *always*. I work with companies who want to put noncompete provisions in place, and I advise them on how to make the noncompete provisions as enforceable as possible. This varies a lot from state to state, but in Illinois, one of the keys is paying separate compensation for the noncompete. If your employer is smart, they're working with an attorney who knows how to draft a noncompete that will survive a court challenge even in a state where courts love to invalidate the agreements.

One of the most common ways a noncompete can suddenly become easy to enforce is when it is coupled to something other than employment. When people say that a noncompete is not enforceable, what they really mean (often without realizing it) is that a noncompete *related to employment* is hard to enforce. Noncompete provisions can be built into agreements that are not strictly tied to employment. If you are presented with an opportunity to become a partner or shareholder in your firm, then you will almost certainly be executing a shareholder agreement or some other similar document. That document may include noncompete provisions, and since that is a shareholder agreement (or operating agreement or partnership agreement, etc.), it is based on ownership of the firm and not just employment. The noncompete provisions in that agreement may be much easier to enforce in court if push comes to shove.

After You've Left

One surprisingly overlooked element of bringing clients with you is the need to be sure that clients can reach you after you've left. Sure, you're going to send your clients a letter announcing your move to a new firm or announcing that you've gone out on your own, and to you, this is one of the biggest moments of your life; but being honest, this is definitely not one of the biggest moments in your clients' lives. They're probably going to lose that letter or perhaps not even open it. At least, in my practice area, my client's simply don't need my services all the time. They call me when they need something, and for many of them, that's relatively rare. So your clients will need a way to find you once you've left.

Often, (assuming you don't do anything ignorant like quitting your job with a same-day notice) your old firm will direct calls to you after you've left, but not always. You're a competitor of theirs now, in fairness. So they may even take a shot at helping a client that calls, looking for you. Business is business. In my personal case, my old firm refused to tell people where I had gone. They even told clients that they had no information about where to reach me. That's their prerogative. Fortunately, though, my clients had other means to find me.

It's important to keep your LinkedIn profile up-to-date and include contact information on that profile. It's also worth your time to *claim your profile* on Google so that people can find you easier with a Google search. Perhaps the simplest thing you can do is to update your e-mail signature with your personal cell phone several months before your potential departure. What did you do the last time you needed to reach someone you hadn't talked to in a while? You almost certainly searched your old e-mails to find them. Obviously that old e-mail address won't reach you anymore, but if your cell phone number is in your e-mail signature, they'll have a way to reach you, and possibly even an entertaining story about your old firm trying to snatch them away from you. Not that I have any personal experience with that…

I am not personally a fan of pursuing clients repeatedly once you've made your move either to a new firm or to go solo. I really don't like the idea of adding prior clients to your new e-mail distribution list. I don't like spamming people with a newsletter that they will almost certainly never read. I don't like being a pest or being annoying. I like simply ensuring that clients know how to reach me when they need something and letting them know I'm available to help them when they need it. My strategy was to simply send the letter, announcing my move to go solo, and then clients contact me as their needs arose. You may want to be more active in your work to move clients over to you, or you may be dealing with a firm working much harder to keep those clients from leaving. So you may need a different strategy. The key is to have an actual strategy and work it as planned. Take time to think through the actual process you'll use to get in front of clients after you've left your job, and be disciplined about sticking to that plan.

The only time I made a second attempt at connecting after I had gone solo was to keep an eye on my client's annual reports. For those who didn't move with me at the time I went solo, I suspected that they may have simply ignored my letter or forgotten about it, but eventually, their corporate or LLC annual report would come due, and that was a good time to reach out to them. This was the case with a handful of clients for me, and when I made that second contact when their annual report came due, it had the desired effect. They confirmed my suspicion. They don't really think about their annual report all that often, and the fact that I had gone solo simply slipped their mind. So when I say that all of my clients moved with me except one, that process actually took about a year to gather them all up.

The main takeaway from this chapter, then, is that you need to start building your own practice today within the firm you're working for right now. You simply cannot assume you'll be able to quit your job, start from nothing, and generate enough business to survive on your own. That's a struggle that no one needs to deal with. First, perfect your ability to sell, and create a book of business while you're still working. Then treat your clients the way you think they should be treated, and build a long, meaningful, genuine relationship with them to ensure that they will follow you when you make your move. Then you will be starting out on your own with existing momentum and existing revenue right from the very beginning.

My only financial concern when I went out on my own was covering expenses during the first month. It actually occurred to me fairly late in the game (i.e., very shortly before I quit my job) that I was going to bill a bunch of clients in the month of October, and they wouldn't even get those bills until the beginning of November. My best-case scenario was to go the first six weeks of my life as a solo without any income at all, and I kind of freaked me out. My solution was to leave my job with about a week left in the month. I walked out of my job on September 21. I immediately contacted my most active clients literally hours after I walked out of my job and lined up work for the last week of September. That way, I had at least a little bit of work so I could send out invoices at the beginning of October. It worked. As noted earlier in this book, October was the first full month on my own, and I made more than I had ever made as an employee.

This is a perfect example of one of those strategies I stumbled into and did in a moment of brief panic, but it's a lesson I think is good when it comes to deciding the timing of your departure. I definitely recommend a mid-month exit to allow you a little bit of time to get some billing in under your new firm before the end of the month.

This entire concept of a mid-month departure highlights my entirely different perspective on going solo, and it's important to pause for a moment. I've said over and over again that the key to going solo is to get your momentum going before you quit your job instead of trying to create momentum afterward. This sounds like a nice concept, and it makes sense, but it doesn't really hit home until you start thinking about how you're going to pay your bills in the first few days and weeks after you quit your job. It's important to notice that my absolute expectation was that I was not going to have a single moment in time where my income is down. I want you to have that exact same expectation.

After I quit my job, I was nervous, just like anyone would be, but there was no gap in my income, and that was no accident. In addition to leaving just before the end of the month to allow for some billing at my new practice, I also had skipped taking a vacation at my job. So in my last paycheck, I received my regular pay up through the last day I worked and almost all of my accrued vacation. So there was no dip in income.

That being said, I also put some safety nets in place. First, my wife was working. If we really needed to, we could barely scrape by on just her income. So that reduced the pressure that was on me, which is important. You want to be sure you can focus on serving your clients and not just grabbing cash wherever you can get it. Second, I took out two loans. One was from a dear friend who had previously been a client, and also, apparently, was an angel. She lent me $10,000 to cover expenses and reduce my stress level right at the beginning. Having that cushion was very stress-relieving even though, thankfully, I never ended up needing that money.

I also eventually took out a $40,000 line of credit when I hired my project manager. I was okay with the thought that I might need to go without a paycheck but was not ever going to have a conversation with an employee where I told them I couldn't pay them. So even though I was careful to set up my transition in a way that resulted in no dip to my personal income, I had these two safety nets in place to allow me to focus on serving clients as opposed to worrying about money.

I can tell you honestly that there is always the thought in the back of my mind that this could all come crashing down, and I'll go broke. However, the income has been steady, and I've never really had a moment of panic about cash. I did eventually use the line of credit, but that was more because I totally failed to manage my taxes as opposed to running short of operating income. I could write another whole book on how un-fun it is to pay taxes as a solo, but we'll leave that for another day.

Up to now, you've solidified your ability to generate business. You've brought in some clients, and you're treating them like kings and queens so they'll follow you when you leave. You've even made some smart moves to be sure that these loyal clients can find you after you've gone. Now you will need to address the main limiting reality that every solo attorney has to face: you have a limited set of skills, but your clients have an unlimited variety of needs. How do you help the people you can't help on your own?

Our next step in setting you up for success as a solo is to put a team into place that can do the things you can't do on your own.

GETTING HELP

Referring Cases and Outsourcing

One of the things that made me the most nervous about going out on my own was losing the backup you have in a firm with attorneys who know other practice areas. My clients have a variety of needs, but I have a fairly narrow focus of expertise. When I worked with a firm, I would walk down the hall to get input or ask questions of other attorneys all the time. Even having other attorneys in your own practice area is nice. It's good to be able to go to someone who does basically the same thing you do to be sure that the strategy you're thinking about makes sense to them. Now, on my own, this is not available unless I'm seeking a second perspective from my dachshund. There is no one down the hall, and if I have a question, I am on my own to figure it out.

Before you go solo, you need to put a network in place to provide backup in these situations. If you play your cards right and don't do anything stupid like quitting without notice, your old firm could still be this support system. If not, you'll need to start building a network of outside professionals who can help you or your clients when you have doubts about how to proceed or are simply not qualified to handle your client's needs.

This begins early, just like everything else described in this book. At least a year before you plan to go on your own, you want to start introducing yourself to other professionals in complimentary practices. For me, this meant finding commercial real estate attorneys, litigation attorneys, personal injury attorneys, and estate planning attorneys. These were the areas that my clients had frequent needs in and I simply didn't know how to do. Fortunately Sean, who we've talked about a bit already, knew commercial real estate law. Don, who is responsible for about half of my success, handles residential real estate law. I met a handful of litigators, and fortunately all of them had slightly different emphases in their litigation practice. So I could pick and choose which cases to send them depending on their specific skill set.

In my opinion, farming work out to people who are well-qualified to handle it is far superior to giving it a shot on your own. Although, not everyone shares this view. I worked at a firm for a while that was somewhat famous for basically saying yes to anyone who called, on the assumption that they were diverse enough in their practice groups that they would figure it out even if no one had specifically handled that type of case before. I was launched into a very awkward phone call as part of this strategy. Our office was only one town over from the local horse racing track. A call came in for someone looking for a transactional lawyer, and it got funneled to me. I was only a few weeks into this new job and barely out of law school, and this potential client asked a very specific question: "Has your firm handled transactions involving horses?" I wasn't sure, being brand-new on board. So I asked around a bit and got a strong yes from one of the partners. Great! I got back on the line with the potential client and reported the good news, and he responded with some hyperspecific horse transaction questions that made it immediately obvious that I had no idea what I was talking about. Who knew that buying and selling horses was so complicated?

The potential client asked politely (but with obvious agitation) to speak to the attorney who had handled horse transactions before. No problem. I was glad to get off the phone. I asked who it was who had handled these types of matters before, and the answer was not what I was looking for: "Well, no one, but it's a sale. Get the client in the door, and we'll bring them in and do a great job."

This was not the answer I was looking for, and it definitely wasn't the answer this potential client was looking for. He was still polite but obviously upset. I believe the word *lying* found its way into the conversation at some point. It was one of the more uncomfortable phone calls I had ever handled, and obviously we never heard from that client again.

This could have gone very differently, and the way it should have been handled is the perfect illustration for why you want to specialize and farm out the rest of your work to other experienced providers. What I should have done is immediately been upfront with the client and told them that we don't handle equestrian transactions (as they are actually called), but that we have a client that I can reach out to whom may know someone. Let me call you back in thirty minutes. This was true. We had a client who spent about half of his time at the racetrack, and he was extremely social. Anywhere he went, he knew everyone. It would not surprise me one bit if he knew people who owned some of the horses that were racing at the track. I could probably have found an attorney experience in the purchase and sale of horses. I could have gained an informed opinion as to whether they seem to know what they are doing and referred the client to them.

Then what? I lost that "sale", right? Wrong. What I gained was an attorney who should feel at least some kind of obligation or desire to return the favor at some point, and the client would have appreciated my honesty. Who knows? We might have even won some of this client's other business as a result of the pleasant experience. Instead, we sent this client off into the world more frustrated than when he had called us in the first place. Not ideal.

Think of the movie *Miracle on 34th Street*. In that movie, we encounter the real Santa Claus who comically ends up working for Cole's as their Santa at the end of their Christmas parade on Thanksgiving. It's an obvious tip of the hat to Macy's. As part of Kriss Kringle's duties, he also acts as the in-store Santa at Cole's main location in New York, and he is discovered to be giving parents advice on where to buy toys *at other stores* if they were not in stock at Cole's or less expensive elsewhere. One of the funnier moments in the movie is when a mother reports this to the store manager, and he replies, "I'm surprised to find that we would be undersold by that much. Where did you learn of this information?"

Her response is the perfect illustration of why I refer out: "From *your* Santa! And if this store believes so much in helping the customer that they would send people somewhere else to get a better price, you've made a customer for life out of me."

At this point, the camera pans over to Santa pointing parents in the direction of other places to buy Cole's products at better prices. It's a funny scene, and it works in law firms too. I refer business to other attorneys all the time. My job is not to bill clients; it's to solve their problems, and if there is someone out there better suited to handling this particular problem, then I owe it to my client to send them there.

When I originally went out on my own, this was my primary concern. What if there is an area of law that I can't handle for a client? I'll have to refer them out, and they'll leave me. It's simply not true if you handle it correctly (more on that below). It has, instead, turned into a significant advantage—quite the opposite of what I was expecting. Instead of sheepishly telling my clients that I might need to refer them out to someone else, it hit me at some point that I was referring cases all along. I was just referring them to someone else in my own firm, and I was limited to referring only to the attorneys that were in my firm. Obviously, any firm that has litigators isn't going to be happy about me referring work out to some other litigator outside the firm, but now, on my own, I have the ability to refer to the best possible litigator regardless of where they work.

I have one attorney that refer simple litigation to. Another handles employment litigation. Another just does ERISA litigation. Another does commercial real estate closings. Another handles complex estate planning. And every one of these attorneys works at a different firm. I can literally choose whoever I want, whoever is best-suited to the task at hand. I've turned the main disadvantage of going solo into a strength.

The best example of this involved an assisted living facility that had a resident who needed to be removed. This resident was significantly impaired, well beyond the ability of the facility to properly care for her. She desperately needed full-time nursing care, which an assisted living facility can't provide. The facility was trying to do the right thing, but the agent (power of attorney) for this resident was a bit unbalanced, to say the least. She would issue aggressive threats or long hate-filled e-mails to the facility about the care they were providing and absolutely refusing to move the resident to a place where she needed to be. This agent would even write long e-mails to the mayor of the town where the facility was located, railing on and on about how poorly the resident was being treated. The facility was genuinely doing their best, but they just weren't equipped to handle this resident's needs. However, this agent was, under no circumstances, going to allow the resident to be moved. It was like talking to a brick wall. I tried and then the long e-mails filled with multicolored, all caps text and threats started coming at me as well.

The matter finally escalated to the point that the agent filed a complaint with the state regulatory agency, and the facility was relieved. Finally there was a venue where this resident would have the opportunity to be placed in an environment that could properly care for her. However, I don't handle these administrative proceedings. Sure, I probably could have figured it out (maybe), but with the life of this resident literally hanging in the balance, I wasn't going to use this opportunity to try to educate myself on handling administrative proceedings on my client's dime. I needed to bring someone in.

At my prior firms, I would have kicked this over to one of the litigators in the firm, but this was a fairly specialized matter. This wasn't just regular courtroom litigation. Honestly, I would have been nervous kicking this out to someone unless they had specific experience in this type of proceeding, but when this case came up, I was on my own. I wasn't bound by a requirement or expectation to keep projects in-house, if at all possible. I could refer this to literally anyone. So I went about finding the right attorney, and the attorney I found was perfect. This guy not only had experience handling these cases, he used to be an administrative law judge hearing cases just like this one. He knew the process inside and out, knew all of the people involved, and knew exactly what to do. He was expensive, far more per hour than I was charging my client, but he was so well-suited to the job that he completed it in an exceptionally short period of time. So despite his higher hourly rate, his bill was a fraction of what most litigators would have charged. He skipped all of the normal long drawn out litigation process and cut right to the heart of what was needed to solve this problem. It was over in literally a few days.

If I had tried to keep that project myself, I probably would have been able to figure it out. Inevitably I would have made some procedural mistakes along the way, but they probably wouldn't have been disastrous. It would definitely have taken me far longer to get it done, so even though I bill less per hour, it would have cost my client much more, and that's assuming it ultimately went okay. What if it didn't? What if this resident died while I was halfway through the process of figuring out how to handle an administrative hearing? This client needed the right attorney on the case, and I wasn't that attorney. By referring this out, the client got exactly what they needed, and I received high praise from my client for finding the right attorney for the job.

Let me go on a brief digression. This is an opportune moment to touch again on the subject of specializing. As noted earlier, if you refer business to someone, they are likely to feel at least some obligation to refer business back to you. However, the attorney handling this unstable agent matter for me worked at a firm that handled just about everything. So he's a bit stuck when it comes to referring business back to me if I'm a generalist. But I'm not a generalist; I focus on a narrow industry: development, management, and licensing of private pay assisted living facilities. That's a fairly narrow focus, and something that no one in his law firm does. So by being a specialist, I make it easier for people to whom I refer business to return the favor.

That being said, don't refer out for the strict quid pro quo. It's great to get something in return when you refer a case to someone, but the key to referring cases out when they are outside your area of expertise is to find someone who is perfectly suited to the task at hand, not just someone who you know will scratch your back after you're done scratching his. Your mission is to serve your client well. That is the action that generates the greatest return. Getting a case referred back to you is just little bonus; it's not the primary driver of choosing where to refer a case.

I take this concept a bit further, and not everyone agrees with me on this. I don't accept referral fees. In the legal industry, it is very commonplace to be paid a fee when you refer a case to another attorney. A typical practice is to pay the referral source one-third or one-quarter of the fees you collect on a case. I don't accept these referral fees. There's nothing wrong with accepting them; it's a topic that is covered specifically in the legal ethics rules in most states, so it's a normal practice. There are specific rules to follow, but as long as you do so, there is no issue. I personally just don't like receiving these fees. I like to be able to tell my clients that I'm choosing the best possible attorney without the inherent conflict of interest involved in also trying to get the best referral kickback.

There are also a lot of hassles involved. Technically, at least in my state, I'm supposed to remain involved in the case, but this rarely actually happens beyond just being copied on e-mails. We also have to disclose the arrangement in writing to the clients, and there is almost always an instinctive reaction to the fact that you just told this client you're sending them to the best qualified person (oh, and by the way, he's kicking a little bit of that back to me. Yay!). I just don't like the optics of it. Finally, I don't really need one more category of information that I need to keep track of and follow up on every few months.

Again, this is my personal preference. I actually pay one attorney a referral fee, and he sends me a lot of business. It's part of his business plan to refer work out and collect these fees, and we play by the rules. We disclose the arrangement to clients, and I keep him in the loop on all of the cases he sends. But for me, I just don't think the extra revenue is worth all of the extra effort required to generate it. It's not really the passive income stream that you were probably imagining at the outset. I would rather just deliver legal services, do a good job for my clients, get paid well for it, and keep my life relatively simple.

You are also going to need to decide what method you use to refer work out. You have two options: you can hand the matter off to the other attorney entirely and watch from a distance, or you can bring the other attorney alongside you, and the two of you work the case together. This should be different for every case you hand out. This isn't something you decide as a general rule for how you run your practice. When I have been heavily involved in a case and there is an aspect of that case that I can't handle, I will bring someone alongside me to work the case together. This works exactly the same way as it does in a law firm when you walk down the hall and ask Joe to help you get a deal closed.

This is particularly seamless as technology plays a larger and larger role in the practice of law over time because it's actually likely that you wouldn't have walked down the hall to see Joe; you would have e-mailed Joe. That's no different than the means I use to reach out for help. I'm just reaching out to attorneys who work somewhere else as opposed to working down the hall. Although, logistically, it's the same. We copy each other on e-mails, we hop on the phone from time to time to go over details of the case, and the client really doesn't see any difference in how the matter proceeds.

A good example of this was a large transaction I had going where a client was purchasing an assisted living center. However, he wasn't really purchasing the real estate; he was actually already a 7 percent owner of the holding company that owned the LLC that owned the real estate. So we just had that holding company buy out the other members, leaving us as the sole member of the whole organization. Pretty slick structure, if you don't mind my saying so, and it was all a bunch of complicated corporate stuff that I love to do. Although, in the end, the client was still going to end up owning a new piece of real estate. So I needed someone to check out the title on the property because I wouldn't know clean title if I bumped into in the shower. In comes Sean (once again) to look over the title and be sure that this parent company we were buying properly owned the LLC and the LLC properly owned the real estate.

In this case, I disclosed that I was bringing Sean on board, and the client consented to it, but other than that one-time consent, I don't think the client even knew that Sean was involved. Sean never e-mailed the client; he only e-mailed me. He never spoke to the client; he only spoke to me. The client also had plenty of other issues to worry about in the lead-up to taking over operations at an assisted living facility. The arrangement worked out perfectly.

This is in stark contrast to another case that came in. Years ago, I helped a client sell their struggling business. It was about as close to a handshake deal as you're going to get. The business was struggling, and we literally sold it to the buyer in exchange for his agreement to take on the contracts that were underway. He paid no money out of pocket for the business. About five years later, my client's daughter calls me in a panic. My client has passed away during these five years, and the buyer has now filed a lawsuit against my client's widow of the old company's bookkeeper.

This was a perfect opportunity to do a full handoff. Other than helping to get the litigator handling the case up to speed, I really didn't have much value to provide on this case. I had my opinion about how it should be defended, but that was the opinion of someone who didn't even know where the courthouse where the case would be heard was located. So once the details of the underlying transaction were conveyed to the litigator I found, I was out of the case, and no, as always, I didn't ask for or receive a referral fee for doing so. I just checked in from time to time to see how the case was going, more out of personal interest than any official legal work. I really like this family, and it bothered me personally that they were involved in a bogus (in my opinion) lawsuit, so I stayed on top of it to see how things were progressing.

With all of this in mind, you're going to want to start identifying who these supporting players are going to be when you're out on your own. You will need to spend time outside of your silo of transactional or litigation or estate planning and shake some hands and meet some people. Perhaps reconnect with some old classmates from law school, or attend continuing legal education seminars and keep track of the names of the presenters who sound like they would be good to work with. In addition to expertise, you also want a good personality fit. You're going to want to find someone who will treat your client and connect with your client in the same way you do (if possible).

As noted, when you do this, you will likely have started receiving reciprocal referrals (especially if you've found a niche and honed your expertise). When this happens, there is a golden rule that can never be broken. Not ever. Don't ever steal the client that is referred to you. If you are brought in on a project to handle something the other attorney can't handle, then you do your project, and you hand that client right back to the attorney who referred the case. You don't add them to your newsletter list. You don't connect with them on LinkedIn. You do the work, and you step back into the background. Poaching clients from your referral sources is not only going to absolutely ensure that you'll never get another referral, but it's just a basic scumbag move that only the lowest of opportunists would pull.

That being said, you need to guard against other attorneys poaching the clients you are referring out to them. Although just above, I've made this sound like a sinister thing that only the lowest of the low would do, it can happen naturally. I mentioned Craig above who handled an eviction case for me that was outside my area of expertise. The client reached out to both Craig and me on a completely unrelated matter, and it was something that I would normally handle for the client. It was also something that Craig could easily have handled as well, but Craig is a stand-up guy, and he did the right thing. He replied to that e-mail, saying, "I'm on top of the eviction, and I think this new matter is something that Jim would normally handle." And that, my friends, is how you ensure you'll get another referral in the future from Jim Voigt.

One problem you will need to manage is that natural tendency for clients to reach out to whoever they were working with the most recently. For this reason, I tend to bring attorneys to work alongside me more often than I do a straight hand-off and back out entirely. I like to stay in front of the client as much as possible (without being creepy about it), and I really do take a personal interest in what is going on with my clients. I will touch base from time to time with the client directly to see how things are going. It's also an opportunity to get feedback on how the client enjoys working with the attorney you brought into the case.

Not every attorney is going to share the bedside manner that clients are accustomed to receive from you, but as long as you know that, it is something you can bring up early in the referral process. "Hey, I'm going to bring Fred Smith in on this case because he works specifically in ERISA litigation, but I need to let you know that clients tend to find him off-putting and dry, but he does good work." These small intros and letting the client know what to expect are important when referring work out to attorneys who will be interacting directly with the client (as opposed to just working through you).

Assembling this outside support team is never really done. You're always going to find new scenarios that require finding someone you haven't previously worked with. Always keep building this outside network. If you're networking correctly, you'll also continue to meet new professionals to consider for future cases. In addition to building your outside network, you will also need to decide how you handle the need for help on the inside. You'll need to grapple with the concept of hiring, when to hire, how to hire, and how to work with the internal team you've created; and, spoiler alert, it's not easy. At least not for me.

DON'T GO IT ALONE

Hire a Support System

When you go solo, you are almost certainly going to need help beyond the network of professionals described in the last chapter. None of those people are going to help you stuff envelopes or improve your operations. You will very likely need to hire an employee (help on the inside), and I am also a strong believer in hiring a coach and/ or working with a mentor (help on the outside).

There is one glaring problem with going solo: you're always right about everything. Sure, that sounds great. No one ever tells you that your ideas are bad, and no one ever tells you that your work process isn't efficient enough. No one ever e-mails you, wondering where you are at two thirty on a Wednesday. These are all the reasons you went solo in the first place. Freedom!

But freedom has a price. I hate to break it to you, Einstein, but not all your ideas are winners, and your work process could probably use a lot of tuning up. Life as a solo is full of possibilities, but one of those possibilities is to completely blow it and not even realize you're doing so.

We've all had that boss at one point or another who thought he could do no wrong. He was always right about everything. If he sought input from his team at all, he never actually implemented their ideas. He worked within his own silo of *greatness*, and your job was basically just to do whatever he told you to do even when you knew for a fact there was a much better way to get the job done.

Going solo is the ultimate definition of working within your own silo. Until you hire staff, there is literally no one else in the room to push back on your bad ideas or to point out that your processes could be better (or in my case, much, much better). As much as I love the romanticized thought of going solo, I have to begrudgingly admit that there are at least *some* benefits to working with other employees. Collaboration is helpful to ensure you're doing the best job you possibly can, and, remember, as a solo, there is no guaranteed paycheck. If you don't do the best job you possibly can, you don't get paid. Since failure is not an option, you're going to need inside and outside help to keep you from going off the rails without even realizing it.

Help on the Inside: Hiring Your First Employee

The primary theme of this book is that you need to put several pieces in place before taking the plunge and quitting your job. You need to develop a book of business. You need to develop your ability to network and market to ensure a strong pipeline of new business. You need to find an outside network of professionals to whom you can refer business and draw upon for matters you can't handle yourself. You need to spend time figuring out what it is you really want from the business you plan to establish, and you do all of this well in advance.

Unfortunately, the critical piece of deciding who to hire to help you internally (an employee) is not something you can put into place before you quit. For most people, myself included, you will likely go solo entirely on your own at first. Sure, employees can help you to be more productive, but they are expensive, and no matter how much risk you are willing to take in your own life, employees don't want to take on the risk of not getting paid. So making your first hire is a bit scary. It adds an element of pressure that is piled on top of the already-substantial pressure of leaving your own regular paycheck. Now you have someone looking to you for *their* regular paycheck. So it is very likely, unless you have a substantial war chest piled up before you go solo, that you'll start on your own and hire later (maybe never).

The need to hire initially is obvious. You need someone to handle the tasks that keep you from billing. The filing. The copying. Running to the post office. Keeping the books. Any task that you cannot bill time for is costing you money. This is the typical (and correct) reason people hire an assistant. However, I quickly discovered another more compelling reason. I discovered that you need a partner, not an assistant.

I've spent a lot of time talking to people who have gone solo, and Matt, a mortgage broker who went out on his own, originally introduced me to this concept that immediately changed my perspective on how to run a solo office. He said, "You don't need secretary; you need a partner." He couldn't be more right. The word *partner* is a very loaded term to lawyers. Don't panic. I'm not referring to the legal concept of partnership. Lawyers are not permitted to enter into legal partnership or split profits with non-attorneys. What Matt meant was that you need to bring someone on board who has the mentality of a partner and not a secretary.

I ended up hiring exactly the right person for this partner role. I was not a hiring genius who came to this realization and then capitalized on my well-crafted hiring strategy. I made this amazing hire the way I make most successful things in my life—entirely by accident.

I had been working on my own for about six weeks. A friend of mine was getting married, but his wife was relocating from out of town. The way he talked about her, she sounded like an absolute go-getter and quite an amazing person. She held two undergrad degrees and a master's degree. She was very successful in high-level sales for large global corporations. She was also an entrepreneur. What a resume!

Obviously, I couldn't hire anyone with a resume like that. I wasn't sure I could afford to hire anyone at all, much less a superstar. As a joke, I sent my friend a text, "Sounds like she'd be perfect to get my sorry butt in shape around here."

He replied, "She would."

Nice little laugh. A cute exchange of text messages among friends, but it left me thinking. Why not ask? I shot him a text message back and said, "I know this sounds crazy, but do you think she might actually be interested?" She was.

The funniest thing about hiring Ami was that her lack of experience in the legal field was exactly what I needed. She was accustomed to operating in a fast-paced sales environment that submitted orders to a well-oiled manufacturing operation. When she told a customer when their order would be delivered, that was a hard deadline, and there was a detailed process put into place to ensure that the deadline was met. Missing a delivery deadline was a major issue to Ami. To me, it was a daily occurrence, and I didn't know how to fix it. When I told a client when I would deliver their project, I had every intention of meeting that deadline, but I had no idea how I was actually going to do so. If Ami had come to me with twenty years of legal secretary experience, she would never have brought the radically different perspective that I desperately needed. She would have assumed that I was the smart lawyer who knew how to get things done, and it was her responsibility to just do what I told her to do.

I didn't know it at the time, but I didn't need someone to stuff envelopes and type letters for me. I needed a hardcore project manager who was intent on delivering projects on time and actively manage my work pipeline. Ami was good at that. Really good at it. Moreover, I needed someone who would push back against my tendency to overcommit and under-deliver. Ami came from a high-level position where people pushed back against one another as needed. She didn't come from a "that's not my job" mindset, or a "do as you're told" mindset; she came from a "deliver what you said you were going to deliver when you said you were going to deliver it" mindset, and that is not common in the legal industry, especially with legal secretaries. Lawyers have big egos, so they don't tend to hire support staff who will push back against them all the time. Ami, however, definitely pushed back.

We came at the concept of productivity from such radically different perspectives that we often tangled. I know that I made her crazy, and she made me crazy. I wanted to start the day at around eight thirty or nine o'clock. She kept pushing it back to seven or seven thirty. This is my business and my house! I'm in charge, right? But the terrible news for me was that she was right. Business was booming, and we just weren't going to get all of this work done if I rolled into the office at nine o'clock. To make things worse, she had this ridiculous expectation that I would work…*the whole day.*

But at the end of the day, we were doing really good work together. Some of the best work I had ever done as an attorney. The key was that I gave Ami genuine authority over my production schedule. In the entire time that she worked for me, I never played the "I'm the boss" card. She respected my authority over the method of getting the legal work done because that was my specialty. I respected her authority over the scheduling and delivery of that work because that was her specialty. It sounds a bit utopian. Many days, to be honest, it was. Some days…not so much. But overall, it worked.

It was scary hiring Ami. We agreed to a salary of $5,000 per month, which is pretty high for assistants in the Chicago suburbs. She wasn't the highest paid legal assistant or project manager or whatever she was. There are legal secretaries making more than Ami, but they have decades of experience. Ami was brand-new at this. She had never even worked in the industry. I was grossly overpaying her for her experience, but I was grossly *underpaying* her for her ridiculously amazing resume. Regardless of what she was worth (which is a concept I kind of hate when applied to human beings), $5,000 every single month is kind of a lot. It's kind of like saying that $80,000 is a great price for a Lamborghini. That's true…but you still need $80,000, and that's a lot of money.

Ami was definitely a Lamborghini, and I was definitely stressing about whether I was going to have $5,000 per month *every month.* I was at the very beginning of my solo career, and this was a seriously high salary for my first employee only a few weeks into going solo. I didn't have a business savings account yet. I didn't have payroll set up. I was still figuring out how to run my billing software. I was grossly underprepared for hiring Ami. However, the results she paid to the business were *almost* instantaneous.

There was a bit of a breaking in period where the very logical Ami had to figure out how the very emotional Jim ran his business. She went into observation mode. She was watching how the work came in, the ridiculous means by which I set my grossly unrealistic delivery deadlines ("Sure, I can get that done first thing tomorrow morning!"), and what was involved in delivering projects. She had never worked in a law office before, and she was absorbing everything like a sponge (and so quickly). She was also pouring through my entire to-do list multiple times each day and slowly came around to making sense of it all while keeping an eagle eye on my e-mail inbox. Every single e-mail in and every single e-mail out. She basically learned the logistics of the business of law and became better at it than I had gotten over the prior fifteen years in a month.

Once Ami got her head around all of this, the results were immediate. My revenue went up by around $10,000 per month, making it easy to pay her salary which was only half that much. Clients were getting their projects delivered faster, so they were happier. Everything was working exceptionally well. I was making basic use of my billing software, but Ami unlocked an entire project management software component that I never knew was there. She had my schedule drilled down to the minute. That became a bit of a problem with my wildly inaccurate estimates of how long projects would take me, but we made progress on that over time, or, let's be honest, *I made progress on that over time.*

As I have mentioned a thousand times, Ami was grossly overqualified and grossly underpaid for her skill set. I knew from the beginning that Ami would only be with me for a short time. Her objective was to learn what needed to be done, put systems in place to get it done in a way that makes clients happy, and leave once that train was smoothly rolling down the track. A train is a good metaphor. They are hard to get moving. A train is a huge object just sitting there, being somewhat useless, but it's full of valuable stuff. Well, valuable if you can get it moving; and getting it moving takes a ton of energy and effort, but once you get all of that moving, it's a pretty profitable business. Ami's job was to get this large freight train all loaded up with legal knowledge moving in a way that was useful to my clients, and she did it.

Around this same time, my wife made the leap from working a well-paying job as a physician's assistant in cardiac surgery to staying home. Knowing that Ami had mostly accomplished her mission, she started working with my wife to hand off operations of the business so that she could move on to something that was far better-suited to her qualifications and skills. After Ami left, my wife and I started working together, and that presented its own unique set of challenges, but we figured it out, and today it's working extremely well. Best of all, I convinced her to push the start of the day back to eight thirty. Jimmy V for the win!

Saying goodbye to Ami was tough, but the process of working out how to keep this business running with my wife by my side has been probably the most enjoyable change in my life ever. I love working with her every day, and so far, she hasn't killed me, which is nice. Still, I keep the payout on my life insurance a little low just in case.

Help on the Outside: Coaches and Mentors

Hiring employees, especially employees like Ami, is a great start, but finding people like Ami to work with you on larger company strategy issues and also handle the mundane day-to-day office tasks is rare. You need to have someone on the outside whose job it is to keep you accountable to your own goals, to provide high level feedback on your business strategies, and to push back when you start wavering from your plans and strategies.

Hiring a business coach or life coach can be invaluable, and it's common among high-performing businesspeople. Not everyone is a huge fan of Oprah, but no one can deny that she built an amazing brand, and she credits some of her success to her life coach, Martha Beck. Or maybe Metallica is more your speed. They attribute much of their success and their ability to accommodate each other's strong personalities to their life coach, Phil Towle. In addition, the "king of the world," Leonardo DiCaprio, seeks out coaching from none other than Tony Robbins. It seems to be working out pretty well for Leo so far.

After my income started to level out, I had some room in the budget to hire a coach. I wanted to be as cool as Leonardo after all. Sadly, Tony Robbins was booked, but I knew a guy, and I had some expectations about what working with a coach would be like. When I think about a coach, the first image I have in my mind is the inspirational high school football coach we see in so many movies. Picture *Remember the Titans*. Coaches genuinely care about their players, and they are relentless in their pursuit of the overall objective. They are incredibly focused, and they have the ability to draw greatness out of their players. They spend about half their time screaming at you and the other half making speeches that bring tears to your eyes. Business coaches and life coaches, however, are…different than that, to say the least.

When I started working with a coach, he immediately started reverse engineering my goals and had this crazy expectation that I was actually going to accomplish all of them (like finishing this book, for example). Personally, I always found it a lot more enjoyable to just talk about all the amazing things I was going to accomplish but then never actually do anything (just ask my former employers). Not my coach. The first thought I had after hiring this guy was, "Oh crap, he actually expects me to do all this stuff I keep talking about doing." I'm a guy who is all about ideas, and I'm a little light on execution. My coach is 100 percent the opposite. He doesn't care what my ideas are; he's here to get me across whatever I decide qualifies as a finish line.

That may not be your need in a coach. Maybe you're a rock star when it comes to executing on your plan, but you're weak on creating that plan. We all have strengths, and we all have weaknesses. You need to find a coach who can identify your strengths and make the most of them. Someone who identifies your weaknesses and presses you to perform around them or through them. Talk to a few different coaches. Don't necessarily pick the coach that agrees with you on everything; look for the coach who is honest with you about everything, even when that honesty is a little bit awkward or painful. The main purpose is to push you and keep you from believing your own BS (either good BS or bad BS) and to remind you of the vision you had when you started out. It's so easy to drift from that vision and start treating your own business like it's just another job. Your coach will keep bringing you back to that vision over and over again and hold you to that vision.

My coach was very vivid in this aspect of his work with me. I mentioned casually one time that I had this idea of writing eventually replacing the daily practice of law as my primary source of income. He started asking probing questions about this vision, and these questions started to really create an image in my mind that I could truly pursue. I started out by simply thinking, "It would be nice to write for a living;" and through working with my coach, that eventually turned into a highly detailed vison of me sitting in a nice home in Sedona, Arizona, with my laptop looking out over the low mountains, typing away and enjoying my dark roast coffee early in the morning with my wife walking over to say good morning, and we enjoy a nice breakfast together. This is far more detail than I had ever put into my vision, and it started truly pushing me to feel a sense of urgency around my writing. Suddenly this wasn't just a nice idea of how I would earn my living; this was a detailed vision, and I wanted it and was willing to work for it.

Then we started engineering that vision. My business was going very well, so the thing that I actually hired my coach to help me with ended up being almost totally ignored by my coach. He dug deep to find out what I really wanted, and that was being a full-time author. Practicing law was just a means to an end to get me there. The law office was cranking along just fine, but the writing wasn't working at all. My book (this book) was going nowhere. However, Chuck identified that weakness and attacked it head-on. I didn't even see that this was a weakness. I needed that coaching to get me realigned with my stated life goal. I could easily have lost a decade or more just coasting through, running my own practice, feeling like an employee all over again, and never finishing my first book.

My health was another issue. As I write this, I'm overweight. I started out about one hundred pounds overweight. Right now,

I'm down twenty pounds from that high point, and I have decent momentum going in the right direction. I credit one mentor and one unofficial coach for that. Rick is a mentor and a good friend, and he'd been pressing me for a while to cut sugar and grains. I knew it made sense, and I halfheartedly did so a few times in my life. But then, David stepped in and made it a bit more real. I went to lunch with David and thought I ordered a fairly healthy meal. Parmesan crusted chicken, garlic mashed potatoes, and green beans. David couldn't eat anything on my plate. The breading on the chicken was a no for him. So were the cherry tomatoes with my green beans (too much sugar in tomatoes). I was surprised, but it opened my eyes.

I didn't go as hardcore as David did in terms of avoiding literally any intake of sugar. But like any coach or mentor, he held a mirror up to my life and I realized that my half-hearted efforts to "reduce" sugar and grains weren't working at all. I saw what it looked like to fully commit, and it was startling. It helped me to set my vision on what I really wanted in terms of health, and the weight started dropping off fast. I didn't go as extreme as David, but I did stick hard-core to my own version of a nutritional overhaul for myself.

I'm not trying to get you to stop eating sugar, but I am trying to get you to bring someone into your life who will act as that mirror to expose the lies and white lies you tell yourself when you're really not pursing your goals the way you could be. You need that pushback, and you need to stay out of your own silo.

Finally, I think you need to pay your coach. I have three great friends who act as mentors to me, but we're friends. I don't pay them, and they don't pay me. They give me great insights into my goals, and they support me 100 percent. I try to do the same for them, but the relationship with my paid coach is 100 percent different. My coach is a nice guy, but his primary objective is not to be my friend. He doesn't have to avoid offending me. Heck, one of his primary missions is to offend me when I need it. And since I'm investing a couple hundred dollars a month on his services, it presses me to stay on track. Why bother paying someone just to make up excuses for why I blew it on my goals each month? If money is tight at the beginning, give yourself six months or a year before you hire a coach, and then stick to that deadline. My revenue has gone up since hiring a coach even though he's not actually coaching me on by business.

You Need a Mirror to Survive

When you are on your own, there is no margin that allows you to perform at anything less than your best. You can cover a lot of shortcomings in a traditional employment environment, but being on your own exposes all the weaknesses. You can stubbornly shut your eyes or embrace your shortcomings, assuming you even know what they are and you probably don't. At least not all of them. Having employees, coaches, and mentors around to help you look honestly in the mirror is one of the most important things you can do as an entrepreneur to avoid allowing these shortcomings to destroy your business.

Before I went solo, I had a very vague understanding that I was a bit emotional from time to time, but it was no big deal. However, one of the friends I noted above said something once that has probably saved my career. I casually said to him once, "Sometimes I think my emotions get in the way of my work." Something like that.

He responded as only a true friend can, saying, "Oh, really? Ya think?"

His tone said everything. Okay, it wasn't a tone. He was laughing at me.

"C'mon, man. I'm not *that* emotional…right?" I asked what he meant.

"Don't take this the wrong way, but you're the most emotional guy I know."

"Seriously?"

"Yeah. Seriously."

Holding this mirror up to me, allowing me to see my true self even though I didn't want to, has probably saved my business. I needed to know that my emotions were a problem, and I never would have without that pushback. I spend a lot of time listening to Tony Robbins, and I've attended a few of his events. He talks all the time about getting your emotions under control if you want to pursue true success. Without that little wake-up call from my friend, I would never have paid attention to Tony's admonition about controlling your emotions, and doing so is probably the hardest part about running by business. Now I'm managing it because I'm aware of it, and I relied on that friend to pushback on me so that I could see it.

There are more practical, less life-altering and less psychological applications for allowing others to help you see your true self. I knew I was a little weak when it came to managing my to-do list, but it wasn't until I saw Ami take that over that I realized this was a massive weakness in my life. I could do a better job of managing my diet, but it wasn't until a mentor of mine dropped forty pounds by quitting sugar that I saw just how out of control my eating was. I always knew I wasn't a huge fan of going through and processing my e-mail inbox, but I never saw how much I genuinely hated it and avoided it until my wife (and project manager) would sit with me while I did it to ensure I didn't veer off into distraction (which is my normal response to something that causes me anxiety).

I started to see my strengths and weaknesses in ways I never could have on my own, and I could start building my business to maximize my strengths and minimize my weaknesses or work to improve them. I saw that I am good at bringing in business, at drafting and reviewing and negotiating agreements, and at communicating with clients and opposing parties and attorneys. That I'm good at closing transactions, and at helping clients find peace in stressful situations. What I'm very much *not* good at is coordinating all of those things into a manageable task list. I can, and do, lose hours every day just managing my to-do list—or more accurately, mismanaging it. I literally cannot decide what task to do next. It's as simple as that. There is too much coming at me, and I succumb to overwhelm very easily. Tell me what to do, and I'll do it well. Force me to choose what I'm doing next, and I'm a disaster.

Ami was instrumental first in the painful process of exposing this incredible weakness. I needed someone who could keep all of these tasks organized for me and help me to determine what required my attention and when so that I could see what it looks like to manage a to-do list properly. This requires the right type of employee. All of my prior assistants treated me like the expert. Sure, I knew more than they did about the law, but when it came to managing my tasks, they were the PhDs, and I was the class clown picking his nose in the back of the class.

Ami held two undergrad degrees in engineering and a master's degree in project management, and she had never worked in the legal industry in her life. She was perfect. I didn't want to replicate the law offices I had worked for before; I wanted to redefine what it meant to practice law. Ami stepped in and created operational systems for scheduling projects, coordinating projects, accommodating urgent projects, and mostly keeping me from considering *every* project urgent. She brought discipline and organization to a business that I had been running almost entirely on my emotions. I felt bad that XYZ client had been waiting on their project, so I did that next without any logical regard for what was genuinely the most pressing project.

Ami was with me for about ten months. It took that long to get my head working correctly to where I could take back the reigns and run the office with just myself and my wife. My wife is not someone who is going to push me as hard as Ami did, so now I'm entering my next phase of self-development. I am taking the weaknesses that Ami helped to expose and correct and taking that to the next level. Now I need to be able to do that without someone pushing me as hard as Ami did, and that's happening. It has its moments, but overall, that improvement is happening. We still run the office today on the foundation that Ami built and the systems she put into place, and we're building on the weaknesses she exposed. If I had been closed-minded to that and treated her like just an employee, I would never have seen the weaknesses that would probably have eventually caused me to fail and go back to my former employer, begging for a job.

The key to understand is that people who work entirely alone have a tendency to miss all of this. We may even operate on a "ready, fire, aim" mentality that has us knee-deep into a new endeavor before we realize we're in big trouble. So even if we have the ability to see our own misgivings, it's always too late when we finally do so. You're going to need some simple support like answering the phone and getting letters copied and into the mailbox, but what you really need is that ever-critical mirror to show you your true self, a self that is very hard to see when working entirely by yourself.

Be Willing to Stretch: Take a Risk

Whether it's a coach or a secretary or a project manager, you're obviously going to be concerned about the cost. When I first went out on my own, I couldn't have afforded Ami. I actually put a line of credit in place to be sure I'd be able to pay her if things didn't go well. I'm not suggesting that you go into debt and hire a top-notch support person regardless of cost, but I am suggesting that you bring someone on board even if it's a financial stretch. It's one of those things where if you wait until you're ready, you'll never do it.

I was not 100 percent ready to bring Ami on board when I hired her. I was paying her about double what a traditional legal secretary for a small firm would be paid. Thousands of dollars per month in a brand-new business where I was still not 100 percent sure I was going to be able to pay myself. I was definitely outside my comfort zone, to say the least, but the results were immediate. At the end of Ami's first full month, my revenue increased by an amount that was more than double her salary. I was working more efficiently than I had in my entire career.

Give Them Genuine Authority

None of this matters if you don't vest some genuine authority in your employees, coaches, and mentors to tell you where you need to grow. My increase in revenue after hiring Ami came because I took direction from her. A lot of direction from her. Don't bother hiring a coach or a secretary or a project manager if you're not going to give them the authority to give you direction that you're actually going to take from them. Yes, you're ultimately in charge. It's your business after all. Ami and I would disagree and sometimes even fight, and at the end of the day, I was the final decision-maker. However, that was exceptionally rare. I gave her the authority she needed over me to put the systems in place that I desperately needed. I do the same with my coaches and mentors today as well.

Be Open to Change

Once you start pursuing your true goals on your own as a solo, you will very quickly uncover all of the buried personal issues you've probably had your whole life, and it's not going to be super fun all the time. Listen to the coaches, mentors, and support people you bring into your life; and be willing to look into the mirror they hold up to your life, whether you like the image in that mirror or not. If you've chosen the right people, they'll work with you to uncover the mess and stick with you to building into something that gives you freedom.

Engage in a Relentless Pursuit of Self-Improvement

One of the main advantages of going solo for me has been the increased time I have to spend with family, but I've also increased the time I spend working on improving myself. Going solo tests all of the aspects of your personality, and therefore does a great job of helping you see the areas where you can use a little help. I mainly address this with books. I read a lot, or, actually, I *listen* a lot. I dive through two or three audio books every month in the pursuit of improving the things about myself that are holding me back from getting everything out of the solo life that I possibly can.

Audio books is just one format. You can follow social media accounts of people who are putting content out every day to help you become a better version of yourself. You can also listen to an unlimited number of podcasts to get you where you need to be professionally and personally. Or all of the above, which is what I do. I mix it up between books, podcasts, and social media posts. For me, it's mainly books and podcasts.

I would encourage you to get through at least one book every month. That's a bare minimum. This is exceptionally easy to do with audio books. I really struggle to find the time and focus needed to read an actual book, but audio books do all the work for you. I *read* while I'm driving (which is rare with a home office) and mainly while I'm getting ready in the morning. Just twenty minutes a day (whether via audio book, old school paper, or e-book) will have you diving through more books than you ever thought possible and absorbing the benefit of all of those words of wisdom.

Don't get hung up on taking every ounce of advice you absorb in these books. Some of it is going to click with you, and some of it is not. Be open to change, as noted earlier in this chapter, but mix this openness to the recognition that you're not an entirely broken person. Don't assume you are constantly in need of a massive overhaul every time you pick up a book that promises to overhaul you.

I never intended for this book to be a list of practical task list of items to help you go solo, like which laser printer to buy or the best brand of pen. Part of the freedom of going solo is deciding those things for yourself. However, I do think that a list of the podcasts and books that have greatly shaped my success as a solo has some value. My favorite and most impactful titles have been:

Books

- Taboo Business Questions: What's Haunting Every Entrepreneur's Growth (Matt Wilhelmi)
- That Will Never Work: The Birth of Netflix and the Amazing Life of an Idea (Marc Randolph)
- Atomic Habits: An Easy & Proven Way to Build Good Habits & Break Bad Ones (James Clear)
- The Motivation Myth: How High Achievers Really Set Themselves Up to Win (Jeff Haden)
- Start with Why: How Great Leaders Inspire Everyone to Take Action (Simon Sinek)
- Relentless: From Good to Great to Unstoppable (Tim Grover)
- The Perfect Day Formula: How to Own the Day and Control Your Life (Craig Ballantyne)

- Man Up: How to Cut the Bullshit and Kick Ass in Business (and in Life) (Bedros Keuilian)
- Awaken the Giant Within: How to Take Immediate Control of Your Mental, Emotional, Physical, and Financial Destiny! (Tony Robbins)

Podcasts

- How I Built This (Guy Raz)
- Empire (Bedros Keuilian and Craig Ballantyne)
- Jocko Podcast (Jocko Willink)

IT'S GO TIME

You Just Ran Out of Chapters

The more time I spend studying success, the more I realize that there are a lot of successful people out there who share my flaws, and probably my biggest flaw is that I get very excited about new projects, but actually starting them, actually taking that first step, is difficult. I start finding ways to distract myself so that I feel busy even though I'm not actually accomplishing anything. Smartphones are excellent tools for this! I encourage you to dive over yours with a tank before you open your own business.

Planning that first step is fun. I wrote an entire chapter about it. However, in that chapter, I also wrote that you can get mired down in the planning phase and stay there forever. Run the numbers and rerun the numbers. Maybe the font on that business plan should be Calibri instead of Times New Roman. Maybe I need just two more new clients before I make the leap aaannnd…two more clients after that. Okay, maybe just *one more client.*

This can go on forever. At some point, you need to take that first step toward going solo. There are a lot of options available. You don't need to do the business plan first and then start teaching yourself to sell and then plan what equipment you'll buy.

We're in the freedom business, remember? At some point, you will need to do something that takes you well outside of your comfort zone. Some people like to start with that thing. Get it over with. There is a great book by Brian Tracy called *Eat That Frog,* and it's all about starting your day with that one task that you've been putting off forever. Just dive in, and get it done. Eat the frog! Yes, it's anxiety-inducing. Yes, it's probably gross, but at some point in time, you just have to do it. So…*eat that frog*. It's a great book. And if you're wired up to want to knock out that worst possible, most anxiety-inducing task first to get moving, then by all means, do so; it's actually the way I finished writing this book.

I was stuck, and I stopped writing for several months. Why? Because I wasn't sure how I was going to finish the book off. I couldn't envision the ending, the final message. I was in a coaching session to get the wheels turning again on writing, and it suddenly hit me. I needed to stop avoiding the process of writing the middle of this book and knock out the ending that I've been stressing about. Basically, do the thing that I've been avoiding for months. So we set out a plan to write at least five hundred words a day in the last chapter for about six days to just get it done. "Write the worst chapter you've ever written." That was the goal. I can always touch it up later. It's up to you as the reader to decide if I've since elevated this chapter beyond the worst-chapter-ever-written. Fingers crossed.

So the next morning, I *ate that frog* and just started typing, and here we are with this book in your hands and this chapter being finally finished. It opened the floodgates for me to write the rest of the book in between. So that's one way to go about this task of getting started and taking your next tangible steps toward going solo.

But what if you're just not an "eat that frog" kind of person? Or what if your personal circumstances don't really allow you to jump headfirst into the thing that gives you the most anxiety? Then the key is that you do *something*. You want to start to build momentum.

The size of your first tangible act as a solo really doesn't matter. It also doesn't need to be a full-on commitment to going solo. I do not recommend a "burn the ships" approach to this process. It could be as simple as touching up your LinkedIn profile to be sure that clients can find you and making sure that you're connected to as many of your clients on LinkedIn as possible. It could literally be as simple as adding your cell phone number to your e-mail signature so clients can contact you after you've left even if all they have is an old e-mail from you. The key is to get some type of action going.

When I quit the first time (the one I got wrong), I did an absolute minimum of planning. Other than actually going out and finding another job, I didn't do much else to plan my departure from the firm I had worked with for eleven years. Remember from chapter 7 that I was angry? This was not a methodical departure. This was the forty-five-year-old version of picking up my ball and running off of the playground (flipping the middle finger back at everyone, as I did so). I burned the ships, to say the least. They won't be sending me any letters, asking me to come back.

Fast forward to the second time I quit my job. I planned ahead and started taking tangible steps toward freedom well in advance of my actual resignation day. First, I stopped asking for guidance from other attorneys in the office. One of the things that stressed me the most about going solo is that there is no one to ask questions of when you're on your own. If you're not 100 percent sure how to handle a situation, you just have to figure it out on your own.[7] So I started doing so even while working at a firm to see how often issues came up where I absolutely needed help from other attorneys. This process was educational and helped me to focus my practice. I had no idea what I was doing when it came to real estate closings, estate planning, and litigation; so I knew that I wasn't going to touch these areas. When those cases came up, I'd bring in specialty counsel or just farm the case out entirely to someone else. Simple enough.

I also started developing a stronger focus as I forced myself to handle projects that I would normally kick out to a younger associate simply because I didn't like doing them. There weren't going to be any younger associates when I was solo, so I had to learn to suck it up and get through every type of project that was within my skillset, whether I enjoyed that type of project or not.

---

[7] Note: In the legal industry, you can't entirely wing it. If something is far outside your area, you should refer it out to another attorney. I can tell you, in my experience, there are a lot of attorneys out there faking it and hoping for the best. That's not a good strategy when going solo. Your clients need your services, not your best attempt at self-education at their expense.

In addition to having other attorneys around me, I was also losing one other exceptionally important factor. I knew that when I opened, I wasn't going to have any staff to support me, so I started training myself to avoid using staff as much as possible. I was typing my own letters, making my own copies, sending my own faxes (back when that was still a thing). I wanted to see what life would be like without an assistant, and I'm glad I did that because it was instrumental in helping me to organize my time and, again, improving my focus.

All of these things I did were good steps to take but were also entirely undetected by my employer. I never announced to my secretary that I was going to stop using her help. She was also assigned to other busy attorneys, so at first, she didn't even notice. She had plenty to keep her busy. I never sent out an e-mail that stated I was going to start avoiding asking questions of other attorneys as much as possible. No. I just quietly, over the course of three months, slipped slowly into a cocoon of isolation for the sole purpose of seeing what it was like. And…I liked it. It was harder, but I liked it.

If you are serious about going solo, look closely at the activities that fill your day, and start to pay attention to the way those activities will be different after you quit. Can you really operate without an office (assuming that's your goal)? Can you really operate without staff support? What equipment do you really need (as opposed to what you've simply become accustomed to)? Can you handle being by yourself all day long every day?

You can make changes in your daily life right now to start to simulate what life will be like as a solo, and you can be subtle about it so that you're not telegraphing your intentions to your employer.

You can also start investigating what you'll need when you're on your own. I decided that I was going to run mostly out of my house but also maintain an office downtown Chicago. So I investigated office space, office sharing, etc. I looked at a used furniture consignment shop for a lawyerly-looking desk and chair, watching their online updates to see when the perfect desk became available. I looked into what type of laptop I would want and printer. I looked at billing and bookkeeping systems that were well-suited to solo attorneys. I looked into what type of support was available to solos who did have questions they couldn't answer on their own. I was already attending networking meetings, but this could be something you try for the first time.

They key is that there is a huge list of tasks you can start to tick off while you're still employed (and still giving your employer legitimate full-time effort). Every one of these tasks that you begin or complete will educate you about life as a solo. I was shocked to find out how much support was available to solo attorneys and how good the insurance and technology options were. I was excited about my new desk and chair. I enjoyed spending time in the evening looking at different laptops.

But you might have a different experience. You may start weaning yourself off of dependence from your secretary and hate it. You may start working with your door closed more often to simulate the rather isolated life of a solo and hate that too. You might look into systems available for billing and bookkeeping and realize that the box office support you've had at your employer is nicer than you thought.

This book is not about twisting your arm to convince you to go solo. Okay...well...the first chapter was exactly that. Guilty. However, the rest of the book is about doing it the right way. Also, going through a transition where you begin to collect reality checks about life as a solo is important because it might cause you to change your mind. You need to be open to that possibility.

I'm not suddenly trying to talk you out of going solo, but a lot of people never even take the smallest first step toward going solo because they aren't 100 percent sure that going solo is right for them. Well, of course you're not sure! You never took even the smallest first step! If you decide that you're not going to take even a single first step toward going solo until you are fully committed to the solo life, then one simple result is almost certain: *you'll never take that first step*. So I'm asking you to take some baby steps without committing to solo life at all. If you don't, you'll end up waiting until you're so fed up with your job that you do something stupid like giving same-day notice that you're quitting your job. Taking these small steps early on in the process all while still giving 100 percent to your employer is essential to ensuring that you are making the right decision. It will either lay down a solid foundation for your solo practice or will reveal that your current job might not be as bad as you thought.

For me, these first baby steps were an absolute magnet toward the solo life. I had great coworkers and some of the most honest and decent bosses you'll ever meet at my downtown firm, so I wasn't being pushed into solo life like so many are. The solo life was pulling me. Hard. I couldn't stop thinking about it.

So let's not assume you're all-in for the solo life. Let's take a few weeks or months or years to start putting pieces into place to confirm it, to be sure you're ready. It's funny because I consider myself a "ready, fire, aim" sort of guy. I tend to make huge life decisions very quickly, and at the time I was deciding to go solo, I felt like this was one of those times, one more thing crazy Jim Voigt was going on a wing and a prayer. But the more I look back on it now, I realize that I was taking baby steps for a long time. I'd been dreaming about it for a long time, taking small steps toward a solo life without even realizing it. So as much as I like the romance of ditching it all in a single moment of inspiration and striking out on my own, I can't make any claim to that romantic and macho strategy. I walked into this life; I didn't run. Heck, I probably *shuffled* into this life as opposed to walking, but I'm glad I did.

Let's flip the coin over. Sure, baby steps might talk you out of going solo, but they might do just the opposite. You might be like me, and every baby step you take toward your goal of going solo will pull you that much more into the dream. Each step might fill you with more and more passion to practice your craft the way you really think you should. To bill what you think is fair. To earn what you think you're worth. To take risks that you know are the right thing to do without the fear and intimidation of a boss or business partner condemning it for you later, and to do so with absolute freedom. Oh, and perhaps the best aspect of the solo life: no meetings.

Kidding aside, I love my life as a solo. I love it with a strong dose of reality. There are nights that I'm working until midnight because there really isn't anyone to farm the work out to. If I don't get it done, my client's wait, and I try my best to avoid that. However, there is a remarkable difference between working until midnight under the threat of a boss who will be furious the next day if you don't versus working until midnight and looking at your billing clock and seeking what you just earned in a single day. That, most definitely, is different than traditional employment.

Still, for me, I think the nonwork reality of going solo has been the most rewarding. I work out of what used to be my living room. My commute is literally zero. I've instantly gained back three hours a day that I used to spend getting suited up for work and commuting forty-five miles into the city, and I love what fills up those three hours instead. On a typical morning, I make breakfast for my wife and I, and we see our eleven- and seventeen-year-old daughters off to school. There is no rushing (depending on when the kids wake up); we have time to cook real food and eat well and drink a nice hot cup of freshly ground dark roast coffee. Depending on the day, I may hit my desk anywhere from 6:00 a.m. to 9:00 a.m.

Last month I took a few hours off in the middle of the day to watch the local high school's homecoming parade. My daughter was in the parade, walking with her teammates, and this was the first time I had seen her in the parade. It's right in the middle of the day on a Friday. I didn't have to send an e-mail to my boss or check with HR or fill out any forms. I wanted to see my daughter in a parade so I went. I woke up a little early that day to get my deliverables out that my client's needed and then closed up shop at around 11:00 a.m. I billed only three hours that day and knew that I wasn't going to walk into work on Monday with an e-mail waiting for me about keeping my hours up. That, to me, is freedom.

No one has given me the judgmental stare for wandering into my office after eight o'clock. There is effort to be sure that everyone saw you were the first one in the office this morning. I don't have to play the game of leaving my light on after I leave so people don't know for sure what time I left (good tip for those of you still traditionally employed).

No one cares about any of the tricks and games we play to give the appearance of dedication to our work except for one group: my clients. I either deliver what they expect or I don't, and their feedback is 100 percent honest. If I don't deliver, don't deliver on time, or don't deliver with quality, they stop calling me. It's a simple system. I am judged solely on the value that I bring to my clients without any office politics or supervisors to impress.

I love the simple honestly of it all. I have the freedom to simply focus on being good at my craft, and I get to define *good* any way that I like. If my clients agree with that definition, then I stay in business. If not, I don't. It doesn't get any simpler than that.

I also like to be able to make mistakes where I am the only one losing if it goes badly. There are two reasons we don't take risks at traditional jobs. One is that we don't want our heads to get chewed off if the risk doesn't pan out. But the other is more genuine. I recently had an important meeting downtown Chicago early in the morning. By coincidence, a good friend had bought tickets for all of us to go see Hamilton downtown, and it was going to get out late. So I decided to stay in a hotel downtown instead of getting home late, only to hike it back to the city the next morning. The most logical hotel to stay in was the one where my clients were attending their convention, and it was over $500 for a night, and I was tired after Hamilton, so I ordered room service. As luck would have it, my clients cancelled their meeting with me the next morning, so technically there was no reason for me to stay downtown at all. But I was being smart and made other appointments that day with clients who live in Chicago. However, Chicago is a big place, and I had no idea that they were so far away. The Uber ride to their home to execute estate planning documents was $50, and so was the ride back to the train station.

In the end, this overnight stay cost me over $1,000. That hurts! And not a single dollar of that actually had to be spent. It was a total loss, except that my estate planning clients really did appreciate the personal trip to their home (they had just had a new baby, and it was hard for them to get out). If I had a regular job, this massive expense would have gotten a stern e-mail, and I would have genuinely felt bad about wasting so much company money. But this was my loss, and my loss only. That $1,000came out of my pocket alone.

I learned a lot that night. I did lose a lot of money, but that loss didn't affect anyone else but me. I put in a few extra hours that weekend to make up for it and recovered just fine.

I've ordered promotional items that were a flop. I've purchased equipment that didn't work out. I've hired vendors that fell short of the mark. I've ordered the wrong toner cartridge (and even broke it trying to install it, so I couldn't return it). I've purchased services I later found out I didn't even need. I've done it all! And I've never gotten a stern look or a passive-aggressive e-mail in response to any of it. It's all just part of learning. Call it tuition, if you like.

The ability to take a risk and be the only affected by the downside of that risk is another form of freedom that I absolutely love. I can try things I would never consider trying if I had to justify it to a boss. I used to spend time stressing over whether I would even present an idea to a boss or manager. No, what the heck? Ready, fire, aim! I'll just come up with an idea and try it immediately. Why not?

Even so, this life is not all roses. There is no one else here to carry the legal work, so there are some late nights. Vacations are hard. On our last family trip to Myrtle Beach, South Carolina, I still billed probably two to three hours per day just to keep up with the work coming in from clients. As a solo, you want to be careful about turning down work or telling clients it will take three weeks to get their project done. When it's busy, you put in the hours and get the work done because you never know when you're going to hit a dry spell.

I'll repeat what I wrote in the introduction to this book. I love this life, and I think it's right for a lot of people. I definitely don't think it's right for everyone, and I don't think solo attorneys are right for every client. My point in this book is to simply open your mind and encourage you to take some safe, manageable steps to investigate the solo life for yourself in small steps. Take these steps in a way that doesn't shortchange your current employer one bit. If you end up walking out on your job, you want to do so with your head held high.

Take some time to solidify your client relationships to be sure they'll follow you. Start to do some marketing to bring in your own clients. If your firm doesn't allow you to do marketing, then start looking for a new job that does. Heck, you may end up loving that job and never going solo. Nothing wrong with that at all. My only caution to you is this: you picked up this book, so you have to admit to yourself that you're curious. Don't be a reckless hero and throw caution to the wind and walk out of your job tomorrow. You owe it to yourself to look seriously into the solo life. You do not want to look back on your life and wonder whether it would have worked out. If you take those small steps to get yourself ready to go solo, and you hate it then, then you've still won because now you know you wouldn't have liked the solo life; you'll never look back in your life and wonder what it would have been like.

If you do decide to take those steps and it draws you in like it did me, then I can tell you that the payoffs are amazing. My income in higher than it's ever been. My relationship with my daughters is stronger than it's ever been. My marriage has changed so much and is so much stronger than it was when we were trudging to and from jobs every day, making other people wealthy.

Overall I still hope you'll take those small early steps and get drawn into a life that tells you, without equivocation, that you are worth far more than any employer could ever pay you.

You deserve every dime of the revenue you generate.

You deserve to spend the time with your family that they need from you and you want with them.

You deserve to grab your laptop and take off to the mountains with your family just because you feel like it and work wherever you can get a decent Wi-Fi connection.

You deserve the validation of having clients say that they love working with you and knowing that it's because you have a unique way of working with clients that just isn't compatible with employment but you know in your heart is right.

Working by your own rules, within your own values, and in the way you feel in your heart is right and having clients flock to you because it is such a powerful reminder of what you were created to be that I hope you will join this solo life and cast off your chains of traditional employment.

There is not a single thing about me that is extraordinary other than the fact that I finally looked inward and saw my own worth. If you can do that, which is not as easy as it sounds, then you can thrive as a solo and enter into a life that you and your family could only have dreamed of while you were an employee.

Welcome to the world of solo entrepreneurship. Now...get to work!

EPILOGUE

I can't thank you enough for taking the time to read through the ideas and thoughts I've provided on the benefits of going solo and the right and wrong ways to go about it. I hope you're able to sift through the wins and losses that I've experienced to build something amazing for yourself. Mostly, I hope that your version of going solo looks different than mine. That's the goal after all—to create something that is uniquely your own.

If you're still in the stages of figuring out if going solo is right for you or you've taken the plunge and have questions and concerns, I encourage you to visit www.iwentsolo.com. There, you'll find weekly posts about my journey of going solo, as well as stories from others who have done so as well. In 2021, I will be launching the *Going Solo Podcast* which posts monthly interviews with attorneys and others who have gone solo and are living their lives by their own design. I'd love to have you on as guest, whether you've gone solo or are just thinking about it.

If you've gone solo, I would love the opportunity to chat with you about your experience and even post an article or podcast about it to help those who are still trying to put the pieces in place.

I wish you the best of luck in your pursuit of a solo career, and remember that the most luck goes to those who just keep moving forward no matter what. God bless you, your business, and your family as you consider the life-changing experience of *Going Solo*.

Sincerely,

ABOUT THE AUTHOR

Founder of Voigt Business Law, LLC, Jim Voigt first went into business for himself at the age of fourteen when he opened Corporate Startups, Inc., to help small businesses launch quickly and efficiently. He has been helping small businesses ever since and has found freedom and success as a solo attorney, focusing his practice entirely on transactional work for small businesses. His years in sales and as an entrepreneur bring a unique perspective to the practice of law, allowing him to excel in business development (i.e., sales) and building long-term client relationships. These are areas where attorneys often struggle, and Jim is passionate about helping other solo attorneys and small firms overcome these struggles to rediscover freedom and joy in the practice of law. Jim offers a variety of speaking, coaching, and mentoring resources through Going Solo, LLC. He has been married to his wife, Elizabeth, for twenty-three years and has two teenage daughters. They live outside Chicago, Illinois.

Learn more at iwentsolo.com and voigtbusinesslaw.com.

CPSIA information can be obtained
at www.ICGtesting.com
Printed in the USA
BVHW032151060721
611334BV00010B/54

9 781636 307725